The Famine Business

The Famine Business

Colin Tudge

Faber and Faber

3 Queen Square London

First published in 1977
by Faber and Faber Limited
3 Queen Square London WC1
Printed in Great Britain by
The Bowering Press Limited
Plymouth

© 1977 Colin Tudge

British Library Cataloguing in Publication Data

Tudge, Colin
 The famine business.
 1. Food supply – Political aspects
 I. Title
 338.1'9   HD9000.6

 ISBN 0-571-10887-3

Contents

Acknowledgements

Almost everybody I know has contributed in some measure to the writing of this book. But I am particularly aware of my debt to Dr K. L. Blaxter, FRS, director of the Rowett Research Centre, Aberdeen, and his colleagues Drs Robin Kay, Bob Orskov, and John Robinson, who first introduced me to the complexities of livestock production in my *Farmers Weekly* days, and have offered much help and encouragement since; to Professor Colin Spedding, of the University of Reading, who taught me the meaning of the word 'efficiency' in agriculture; to Professor N. W. Simmonds, FRS, director of the Scottish Plant Breeding Station, Pentlandfield, for his help in understanding crop production, and general encouragement. I am also grateful to Dr Hugh Trowell, and Dr Ken Heaton, of the University of Bristol, for their help in framing the comments on nutrition. Mr W. J. Dempster, FRCS, of the Royal Postgraduate Medical School, London, has offered continual and invaluable assistance in providing the historical and political perspective of Chapters I and III. For help on the politics, too, I am grateful to my friends Mark Robinson, and to David Miller, Fred Kavalier, and also to Dr Geoffrey Watts – who read and helpfully criticized vast chunks of manuscript, and was usually abused for his pains. And I should like to thank my friends and occasional colleagues at *New Scientist* for their encouragement, in particular Dr Bernard Dixon, who first suggested I should write this book, and Ian Low, who first led me to believe I could do it.

Finally, I must acknowledge my debt to Dr Michael O'Donnell, editor of *World Medicine*, without whose support I could not have written this book at all. And my thanks to Marianne Noami and Rosemary, my wife, who typed it.

Is There a
World Food Problem?

The most startling aspect of the world's food problem is not the statistics, though the United Nations say that more than 400 million people are underfed; nor the prognosis, though the world's population will double in the next 30 years, and production is often failing to keep pace. It is that we are perfectly able, technically, to feed all the people well for at least the foreseeable future; we even have the necessary goodwill; and yet we pursue policies and encourage techniques that will make our real but man-made crisis worse.

And by 'techniques' I imply nothing very spectacular. The lagoons of protein-rich algae, or the factories of nourishing bacteria that the technophiles dream about and are developing, should never do more than supplement good farming, and certainly should not – as sometimes now seems to be the case – be developed at agriculture's expense. 'Feeding the people well' does not imply crude nourishment or newfangled formulae. Traditional cuisines, which we love because we have grown up with them, and which have a central role in all cultures, can meet our needs.

But we must re-think. We must begin again from first principles. Accept that the problems we now face are different in kind as well as in magnitude from anything mankind has faced before. Accept that many of the policies we now pursue so vigorously originated under conditions that no longer pertain; that many of our ambitions, too, have become inappropriate. I have sometimes been accused of being 'unrealistic', because I suggest that some of our gaudiest band-wagons – including much of the modern food-processing industry – are leading us to destruction, and must at least be re-directed. Yet it seems to me far more 'realistic' to analyse the food problem as it really is, and to ask which of our aspirations are tenable and which are not, and then to devise policies that meet those feasible aspirations, than slavishly to assume that the institutions and conceits we have inherited must be propped up at all costs. If this book at times seems revolutionary, it is because revolution, in some contexts, is necessary. But revolt in this book is usually directed only against our more bizarre bureaucracies, or our more euphoric flights of technological fancy.

The groundswell of each country's culture is not a fit object of revolution, but should form the basis of future policy.

So let's start from first principles. At the World Food Conference, held in Rome in November 1974, the United Nations said that of a world population of 3·7 billion (3,700 million), at least 460 million were conspicuously ill-fed;[1] and the UN could have added that at least another 600 million are constantly on the edge of mal-nourishment. In 34 developing countries – 25 per cent of all the countries in the world – food production between 1952 and 1972 did not increase as rapidly as population. The world food problem was, said the UN, 'the greatest crisis mankind has faced'.

Yet, oddly, the crisis came as a surprise. The 1960s brought good harvests, augmented by the Third World's 'green revolution', based on American-developed dwarf strains of wheat and rice. The world's food problem was not shortage, apparently, but over-production, leading to low prices and agricultural depression. The US took land out of production, and in the early 1970s both the US and Canada ran down their grain stores. Then the bad weather of 1972 brought dismal harvests to the USSR, China, India, Australia and the Sahel countries south of the Sahara. Russia bought massively on the world grain markets before others, including the US, realized what was happening. By mid-1974 there was only enough grain left in store to feed the world's population for three-and-a-half weeks; terrifying brinkmanship. World prices of white rice increased four times between 1972 and 1974, and wheat prices almost doubled.

The World Food Conference helped: it left behind the World Food Council, with new powers to survey the scene and influence the flow of resources. But it showed too that a few countries – like the USSR with its incontrovertible five-year plans, and the EEC, fussing over its butter mountain – could ride out major agricultural disasters perfectly well, even though others starved on an unprecedented scale. And it raised three outstanding questions: why, if this is so, should the rich countries care? Second, is there anything to be done, or has the Third World simply bred beyond its capacity? And third, if the Third World people can be fed, why aren't they? Why are they so vulnerable to one bad harvest?

One answer to the first question – why should the rich care? – is that the Third World is growing in strength, and that by terrorism (given a nasty edge by nuclear weaponry) or commandeering its own assets as OPEC has done, it could make life increasingly uncomfortable for the rich. But it is hard to see how terrorism could benefit countries that seek western friendship or those, like Tanzania, that prefer to work out their own salvation. And no other commodity has the unique value of oil, and no other region the pivotal geographical position between the superpowers, that give the OPEC countries their strength. The rich countries probably need not concede if they choose not to. In truth, the main reason for wanting to solve the world's food problems, which primarily are the Third World's problems, is politically the vaguest and least convincing: that to live in a world where some seek ways of jettisoning wealth while others starve is intolerable, even if we are on the winning side. The decision to exert ourselves is fundamentally one of ethics, and all other arguments are subsidiary.

But if the world's food problems are worth solving, what must be achieved? One thousand million people in the world today are under 14 years of age, and because of this the world population will double, barring mass disaster, by AD 2000, however vigorously population control policies are pursued. So the imminent task is to feed seven billion people. Can this be done?

The Russians suggested at the World Food Conference that the world could support four times the present population – 12 to 15 billion – which seems a reasonable compromise between the unjustified pessimism of those who suggest the world is already over-populated and the euphoria of those who say that if all world agriculture worked as beautifully as it does on a few well-favoured farms, and if protein factories mushroom as quickly as they have in the past few years, we might feed ten times that number. But the possibilities of error are so great, and the consequences of error so total, that we can be sure of feeding the pending population of seven billion only by food policies specifically designed to feed people. You may think that too blindingly obvious. But in recent history, such policies have been rare.

And those food policies, as suggested above, must revolve around agriculture. The new protein factories that the major oil and chemical companies are developing, and which cultivate yeasts or fungi or bacteria on industrial – usually oil – by-products are extremely expensive, and perhaps can be afforded only by those countries that do not need them, at least where 'need' means feeding people rather than pigs. Their raw material – oil – will one day run out, whereas the sun, the basic energy source of agriculture, will not; and the sun provides the world with more energy in three days than could be produced by all resources of fossil fuel known at present. And the new factories depend, in general, on a few technocrats, yet the world will have labour in super-abundance. The protein factories will find a role, which in a few odd niches might even be a crucial one. But they can and should only supplement farming; they are not a panacea.

The sea, too, is probably not the cornucopia that marine biologists once suggested. At present fish, and the rest, supply only 2 per cent of world protein needs, and some of the world's most productive fisheries are already under strain. With careful management (of which there are too few signs) and by utilizing species at present under-exploited (notably the squid) we might increase the sea's yield one and a half to four times, on a sustainable basis.[2] But we are still talking about a marginal resource.

So let's talk about farming. We face two major constraints. That the fuels vital for tractors and for making fertilizers will one day run out; and that the world cannot be made any bigger: we have only so much land. We must devise an agriculture that uses fuel and land conservatively.

Which the dominant and trend-setting agriculture of the west does not. Primitive farmers, fertilizing by manure and cultivating by hand, produce 5 to 50 calories worth of food for every calorie they expend, while the industrialized systems of the west put in 5 to 10 calories, primarily of fossil fuel, to obtain one food calorie in return.[3]

This statistic is not that alarming. After all, by using tractors instead of horses Britain has increased its effective lowland area by about one-third during this century – simply by releasing the land once used to feed horses. And whereas Britain had a million horses at the turn of this century, the US peaked at 22 million in 1920; one small example of how the judicious use of oil can lift a massive load.

And though lack of oil or oil products is now causing Third World hardship – shortage of nitrogen fertilizer, which needs oil for production, is said to reduce the Indian wheat harvest by about 10 million tons a year – it is ludicrous to suggest that fuel shortage, *per se*, is responsible for the world's food shortages. Britain and the US, for example – the latter the most energy-expensive agriculture in the world – use less than three per cent of their total energy on agriculture. And if India is short of fertilizer, the world as a whole is not: the US puts more on its tennis courts and lawns than India, with almost three times the US population, uses for all purposes.

Yet western food production does use energy too profligately. For the agricultures of the US and Britain are only part of a system in which most of what is grown is processed before it reaches the table.

And if you add the energy cost of processing, and the fact that about half the trucks in the US are shifting food from specialist farm to factory to centralized hypermarket, you find that the US uses almost 13 per cent of its total fuel on food production, and Britain, almost 16 per cent. If the Indians produced food the US way, and if they increased their present inadequate food intake of 2,000 kcals per day to the US level of 3,000 kcals, they would have to use more energy for food production than they now use for all purposes; and to feed the whole world by the methods of the US would require 80 per cent of the world's total present energy expenditure. Western-style agriculture, for all its spectacle, does not provide a suitable model for the rest to follow.[3]

For fuel has not been used simply to replace work animals, which is worthwhile, or to decrease human graft, which is desirable, but also to eliminate many of the subtle but expensive skills of husbandry, which only human beings can carry out. Thus the proportion of the population employed on the land in the US halved between 1920 and 1950; halved again by 1962; and had almost halved again by 1974 – with more than half the remaining farmers holding other jobs as well. Even this 'saving' is largely illusory, since every US farm worker is now backed by two 'support workers' – mechanics, advisers, and the rest. As John S. and Carol E. Steinhart commented in *Science*:[4] 'yesterday's farmer is today's canner, tractor mechanic, and fast-food carhop.'

The crux is that to use energy to abet husbandry – and a tractor can plough what a horse cannot – is useful; but to use it to replace husbandry is to squander it. Thus while Britain's agricultural output doubled between 1900 and 1970, her use of nitrogen fertilizer increased about eight-fold, and of potassium and phosphorus, about 30-fold. And once you add in the land saved by the demise of the farm horse, you find yield per acre, despite this massive use of fertilizer, has increased only about 50 per cent.

A clue to what might have been achieved if Britain had used all that energy only to help her farmers, and not also to replace them, is given in a study made in 1951 of 600 gardens in London suburbs. This showed, as Gerald Leach reports in *Energy and Food Production*, 'that the financial output of food per unit area for the average house-and-garden plot was very close to that for the best farmland (£42 and £45 per acre respectively) and substantially higher than for the average (£36 per acre)'. Yet 'only 14 per cent of the house-plot area was actually used for growing fruit and vegetables'. The average output of these plots 'on a mere 250 sq metres, are sufficient to provide all the protein needs (at 54 g a day) and one third of the energy needs of the average Britain, albeit on an all vegetable diet'. Energy expenditure was fairly high, but about 70 per cent was used for artificial fertilizers – which 'could certainly be reduced by recycling vegetable wastes as composts and green manures'; and less than 10 per cent of the energy used in conventional US and British agriculture is used to nourish the crops. I am certainly not suggesting – as later chapters will make clear – that we, or the rest of the world, should base our agriculture on a patchwork of garden plots. I want only to emphasize that to use fuel instead of husbandry can of course save money in the short term, since a calorie of oil energy is far cheaper than a calorie of man energy; but when you channel that fuel energy through the skill of a husbandman, you can raise productivity into a new league.

What of land? We have three courses, in theory: to exploit new areas, to increase productivity of the land we have, and to use agricultural land specifically to grow food for humans, which at present we do only in part.

The search for completely new agricultural areas is more or less over. Plans to farm the Amazon basin, for example, should be treated with extreme caution. The aesthetic objection to eliminating one of the last great areas of natural beauty is obvious; but also, such tropical rain forest, for all its showiness, is highly precarious. The top soil is only a few inches deep, ready to blow away when its cover has gone, and the lush growth is largely water, disguising an inherently low level of fertility. India's recent cycles of flood and drought have been attributed in part to too rigorous deforestation.

Schemes to reclaim deserts are worth taking seriously, but the scale is vast. Georg Borgstrom has pointed out[5] that to pump up groundwater to irrigate the plains of Southern Texas (to take a fairly modest example) would require 15,000 plants, 'in effect larger than the present chemical plants of the present day United States'.

We have mentioned one aspect of increasing productivity of the land we have – by husbandry – and it is worth noting that even the most orderly houses need putting in order. In Britain, which in cash terms claims to have 'the most efficient agriculture in the world' we see farms which should be mixed if production were the aim, geared to monoculture to make better use of machines; micro-habitats, a million favoured slopes and valleys, left out of account for want of husbandry; vast areas poorly drained; water supply mostly left to the hazard of weather; and the hills virtually abandoned – to sheep, whose productivity, again for want of husbandry, rarely approaches that of Iceland where conditions are harsher and sheep are taken seriously. In short, even in the best-run agricultures, and even without considering the kind of re-structuring proposed in this book, there is enormous room for improvement.

And we should, if we take the world's food problems seriously, use the best land to grow human food. World-wide, 250,000 square miles (64,750,000 sq km) – one and a half times the area of California, enough land to feed the world's present hungry people several times over – is given over to 'cash crops' like coffee, tea, cocoa and the rest, which may have little or no nutritional value.[6] More significantly, much of what does have nutritional value, in particular cereals and beans, is fed to livestock, which squanders about 90 per cent of the original vegetable protein. Britain gives two-thirds of its home-grown cereal to livestock and if the land used to produce this grain were used for human food, Britain could theoretically support 250 million (five times its present population) on an all-vegetable diet, even using present agricultural methods. The rich countries (including the USSR) give more grain to livestock than is consumed by the whole of the Third World, people, livestock and all. In the face of such prodigality, the various technological talismans, from bacterial protein to uprooted Amazon forest, are revealed as the diversions they are.

In general, if a country like Britain elects to grow only half the food it needs – as it does – then it places the burden of growing the other half elsewhere. It has been more profitable – 'economic' – to grow only half our food, which is why we do it. But in a world where people are already hungry, in which population is bound to double, and in which we are within sight of physical limits, we must surely ask whether our simplistic registers of cash flow meet the case; whether a re-assessment from first principles is 'unrealistic', or vital.

Plenty of scope, then, to use land and energy more conservatively and productively; no reasonable doubt that we could, if we chose, provide enough for the seven billions. But what is the point? If population continues to double every 20 years or so, as it would if the present growth rate continued, then it could theoretically touch 30 billion by AD 2040, within the lifetimes of many people now alive. Few have suggested that we could accommodate that many. But by striving to keep abreast of growth, to accommodate the immediate prospect of seven billion, are we not merely postponing disaster? Will we not have to face even greater, less tractable famines, in a generation or so? Is the present concern for the world's hungry more

than effete liberalism, storing up trouble for our children while we
salve our own consciences?

The spectre of 'overpopulation' brings out the worst in people;
induces muddled and simplistic thinking; excuses ruthless policies
as 'realism'. Certainly the idea that we should strive to support a
human population as large as the world could physically contain seems
pretty unwholesome. Life would surely be intolerable if everyone were
constantly aware of physical restraint. It is reasonable to hope and
contrive to help world population level out long before the theoretical physical maximum is reached. But we need not allow starvation
to determine the cut-off point; indeed, to sanction privation as a
means of controlling population growth is paradoxically to encourage
that growth, and to preclude the more rational means whereby the
growth could be contained. To allow people to starve to death is not
only a ruthless means of controlling numbers; it is also self-defeating.

The English cleric Thomas Malthus, who published his *Essay on
Population* at the end of the eighteenth century, began, or rather made
respectable, the still-prevailing fear of 'over population'. Charles Dar-
win reinforced his thesis, arguing in his *Origin of Species* (1859) that
it was overproduction among all species that led to competition, and
competition that led to evolutionary change; and the fact that animals
have evolved, the herbivores grown fleeter and the predators cleverer,
seemed to prove the case. So, more immediately, did the politics of the
day. The beginning of the nineteenth century in Britain saw the birth
of the industrial revolution; it also saw a spectacular growth in human
population; it also produced privation on a scale that the intelligent
middle class had rarely been obliged to witness. Obviously the people
were overbreeding, and thus causing their own downfall. Clearly,
as Ebenezer Scrooge commented in Charles Dickens's *Christmas Carol*,
it was necessary to lower 'the surplus population'. But the most
significant fact about Thomas Malthus was that he did belong to the
eighteenth century. He was an armchair philosopher, content to spin
high-flown theory from the evidence he could gather from his manse
window. Moral philosophers do not now quote David Hume as the
final arbiter of human ethics; no more should biologists and politicians
continue to flaunt Thomas Malthus.

For the truth is that human beings do not, necessarily, breed to
the limits of their environment; population is not, necessarily, curtailed
solely by war or hunger. This has happened many times, but it is not
an inescapable biological phenomenon. The generalizations that do
hold are first, that different populations breed at different rates and in

general, given time, adapt their breeding rate to the prevailing conditions. And second, that at times – as happened at the beginning of Britain's industrial revolution, and as is happening now in the Third World – the conditions have changed so fast as to make the established breeding pattern inappropriate. But Britain's rate of population increase began to fall off around the beginning of this century, some generations after industry had become a fact, but long before contraception had felt the gentle hand of science. And there is no reason to think birth patterns in some of the modern underfed countries cannot adjust, when conditions are right.

The evidence that population adapts to conditions has been summarized by Professor Don E. Dumond, in *Science*.[7] He points out, for example, that although the Kung bushmen of the Dobe area of Botswana are obviously potentially very fecund – and do breed quickly if their numbers are reduced by epidemic – their total population is far smaller than their environment could support. Life expectancy is to more than 30, and 60 per cent survive to age 15; there is no sign of mass starvation among superfluous infants, as Malthusian theory would have us expect. By various means – and chastity may well play a part – such hunting and gathering people keep their birth rate down. It simply is not possible to cart a lot of children around if you are nomadic.

But farming communities, without modern technology, need a lot of people. Agrarian societies accordingly adapt, with a high birth rate. The loose family structure of such societies, children working alongside parents and uncles in the field, also militates against the nuclear family, in which a large number of children are highly conspicuous.

But when the agrarian society becomes industrial, and the families, now urban, become nuclear, such fecundity is no longer appropriate. And birth rate does fall. Although, as happened in early nineteenth-century Britain, the birth pattern that had become habitual in the previous agricultural age, does persist for a time.

If you apply Malthusian speculation to the present Third World population explosion, you conclude, in common with many politicians, that people are now producing more children than they can support simply because modern medicine is allowing more and more infants to live. That is a factor. But modern evidence from population data, as opposed to Malthus's armchair, suggests that this high birth rate is primarily an adaptation (and can re-adapt). It is an adaptation, first, to agrarian life, since most Third World people have been agrarian for many, in some cases hundreds, of generations. But it is also an adaptation to poverty, and in some cases to political or social oppression. It may seem paradoxical to breed when you are poor; it is not if you really are poor, within a poor society, when children are your sole possession, and your sole insurance for your old age. Unquestionably we need population control policies providing people with technical aids to control birth rates if they choose to. But the crucial component of such policies is motivation; and motivation implies creating conditions in which large families can be seen to be inappropriate.

In short, if we want to control world population, whether at four billions, or seven, or twelve, then we must ensure that the people who have the babies want to control their births; and the only way to do that, so history suggests, is to create a degree of physical and political security such that a mass of children is no longer seen to be necessary. We could keep the world population at seven billion, or thereabouts, not by allowing people to starve, but only by ensuring they are well fed.

In truth, ruling minorities have been complaining about overpopulation for centuries — as in sixteenth-century England, when the peasants were cleared to make way for sheep; and as in eighteenth- and nineteenth-century Scotland, when the Highlands were 'cleared' for the same reason. But the only generalization that held then, as now, is that the economic system of the day simply was not designed to accommodate all the people. In 1948 many western intellectuals predicted that China's revolutionary government would fail because China's population, 400 million, was too great; now China has 800 million and mass famine is evidently past. China, incidentally, is a great advocate of the slogan 'look after the people, and let population take care of itself' — though it has pursued the most thorough and effective population control policy in history. But China has demonstrated that the prime task is to adjust agricultural policy to the people who need to be fed; and not, procrusteanly, to complain that the population does not fit in with the policies that happen to be most convenient.

So we have enough resources easily to feed the present population, and that of a generation's time: and we can reasonably hope for world population to level out before it is merely cut down by starvation. But we cannot continue indefinitely to squander on the scale we do, and cannot expect new technologies (like tidal electric power, or, indeed, the microbial protein factories) to compensate for profligacy; at best, they will help us to be conservative. More, the present world scene is characterized by staggering inequity, such that the average US American gets through about 1,800 lb (820 kg) of grain a year, but eats only 200 lb (90 kg) as grain, the rest being passaged through livestock, while the average Third Worlder gets about 500 lb (225 kg) a year, mostly eaten in a pristine form; such that one-tenth of the grain given to beef cattle in 1974 (and beeves eat far more grass than grain) would have met the entire Asian shortfall; such that 15 per cent of the world's population expropriates 75 per cent of all fertilizer.[8] This inequity is a legacy of past competitiveness; and so long as we tolerate it, or indeed use others' poverty as a means of exerting power over them, then some people will always go to the wall no matter how many new resources are mobilized. The devil will always take the hindmost.

So we emerge with two simple ideas: that the rich countries cannot continue indefinitely with their dream of seemingly limitless material 'growth'; and that they should curb their aspiration largely in order to give poorer countries a bigger share of the action. But to suggest that the rich should go easy to give the others a chance is to evoke the kind of comment Henry Kissinger made at the World Food Conference: 'All nations – east, west, north and south – are linked to a single economic system.' All nations, he asserted, warm themselves at the same economic hearth. The west may be a little extravagant, but in consuming it creates trade and fosters industry. If we cooled our material aspiration, we would douse the world's economic fires and the resulting depression would harm everybody, including, or perhaps particularly, those poor countries that now rely on intercourse with the rich. In short (according to Kissinger and, indeed, most of the rich governments) to talk of equity in the sense of spreading present resources around is to talk simplistic nonsense. The poor need the rich to stay rich.

This is an ancient argument. Menenius used it in *Coriolanus* to justify the patrician ascendancy over the unruly plebs. And this ascendancy, said Menenius, was not merely material; the patricians were the conscience and the soul of Rome: 'We . . . are the brain; you are the belly.' Not mere aristocrats, but moral leaders. Or as Lyndon Johnson put it, 'The people of the world . . . are looking to our system to show them the way into the twentieth century. And we must not fail because the alternative is anarchy and through anarchy the enemies of freedom will triumph!'[9] So it is sad that so many people should starve; but really it is in their long-term interests to keep the present system afloat.

And of course many Third World countries have relied and do rely heavily on the patronage of the rich – specifically, on aid, trade, and foreign investment. But do they really benefit, in net, or do they, like Rome's plebs, pay too heavily for their tenuous security? And what is the long-term aim? What kind of future is supposed to justify the present misery? Should the Third World countries really aspire to become more like the present rich countries – as the euphemistic term 'developing country' seems to imply? Or are they, in following our lead, progressing down a blind alley?

Well, let's look at aid: a post-World War II phenomenon, though it may seem to have been in the political vocabulary for ever, and largely dominated by the US. According to President Johnson, the US Foreign Assistance Programme 'still stands as a pioneering humanitarian effort without parallel in all of history'.

The US has as much claim as any country, and more than most, to be called humanitarian. But aid has evolved, and is used, as a means of spreading US influence and of balancing its agricultural books; agriculture is the backbone of the US economy and has had constantly to shake off the spectre of overproduction. In practice, Laos, Cambodia and Vietnam have been among the chief recipients of aid; and it is not cynical to suggest that the well-being of individual South-East Asians was not the chief motivation, nor to suggest that US involvement in South East Asia has sadly delayed what could have been a spectacular economic development. As Senator McGee said in 1965, 'that empire in South East Asia is the last major resource area outside the control of anyone of the major powers of the globe . . . I believe that the condition of the Vietnamese people, and the direction in which their future may be going, are at this stage secondary, not primary.'[10] And the 'aid' was an integral part of US involvement, justifying and abetting the military.

But if we admit Vietnam was a failure, Taiwan, another of the chief recipients of aid, has surely been a success. Yet, as C. R. Hensman suggests in *Rich against Poor*, 'the assiduous advertising of Taiwan, dominated by an expensive and unproductive police apparatus of which its citizens live in terror, as a model of what international development can achieve, calls for more discussion of the kind of society the US, Britain, Japan, and other affluent countries would like to "develop" in the Third World'.

Politicians now talk more soberly of aid than Lyndon Johnson used to do. The British, at the World Food Conference, emphasized that it should be regarded as a short-term expedient, with the long-term aim of helping the recipient stand on its own feet. Even the Chinese, world symbols of Third World self-help, said, 'of course self-reliance by no means implies self-seclusion or refusal of foreign aid'.

But we can see that aid is truly beneficial only under somewhat delicate circumstances; only when the donor humbly accepts the right of the recipient to go his own way, perhaps in future becoming a trade competitor, and not simply a satellite. The mere donation of 'aid', the mere fact that only the rich can afford to offer it, certainly does not imply that a poor country necessarily benefits from the rich country's affluence.

Trade has a more respectable feel than aid; it implies two-way traffic. The Chinese told the World Food Conference: 'We have always held that on the basis of mutual respect for state sovereignty, all countries acquire the food they need through trade and make up for one another's economic and technological difficulties.'

But the key phrase is 'mutual respect for state sovereignty'; and this certainly does not, and has not, characterized trade between rich and poor countries. For a start, the role of exports in Third World economies is quite different from their role in 'developed' countries. Western businessmen regard the foreign market as a complement to the home market: the foreign market is more flexible and acts as a buffer, particularly to take up excess; the home market provides the stable base. But foreign sales are not merely a back-stop for Third World economies; they have become the life-line. For example, the US is the world's biggest exporter of soya, but still exports only 28 per cent of its crop; while Senegal and Nigeria put 80 to 90 per cent of their groundnuts on to the world market. To be so reliant on others' willingness to buy is to be in a very weak bargaining position.

And the Third World countries traditionally export raw materials, while western countries export manufactured goods, with much higher value and flexibility of price. The myth is that we have the 'know-how' and 'they', being backward and underdeveloped, are best left to provide the tropical climate and cheap labour. But the tradition did not arise primarily because of innate differences between the people of the present rich countries and those of the poor. It has been assiduously cultivated over 400 years, to provide us with exactly the kind of affluent ascendency we now enjoy – as a cursory glance at British involvement in India reveals.

When the British East India Company was founded in 1600 India's resources were already famed and widely coveted in Europe. In 1660, before the break-up of the Mogul Empire, the French traveller Bernier wrote of Bengal in these terms:[11] 'The knowledge that I have acquired of Bengal in two visits inclines me to believe that it is richer than Egypt. It exports in abundance cottons and silks, rice, sugar, and butter. It produces amply for its own consumption of wheat, vegetables, grains, fowls, ducks and geese. It has immense herds of pigs and flocks of sheep and goats. Fish of every kind it has in profusion.' And, 'from Rasmahal to the sea is an endless number of canals, cut in bygone ages from the Ganges by immense labour for navigation and irrigation.'[12]

In 1757, the year of the Battle of Plassey, traditionally taken as the beginning of British territorial rule, Robert Clive said that Bengal's capital, Murshidabad, was 'as extensive, populous and rich as the City of London'. And as the Indian Industrial Commission of 1916–18 acknowledged,[13] 'when merchant adventurers from the west made their appearance in India, the industrial development . . . was not inferior to that of the more advanced European nations'.

So why did India fall so disastrously behind? Here is William Fullarton, M.P., writing about Bengal at the end of the eighteenth century[14] when Britain's industrial revolution was about to take off: '. . . such has been the restless energy of our misgovernment that within the short space of 20 years many parts of these countries have been reduced to the appearance of a desert. The fields are no longer cultivated; extensive tracts are already overgrown with thickets; the husbandman is plundered; the manufacture oppressed; famine has been repeatedly endured; and depopulation has ensued.'

For it was not in Britain's interests to treat India with 'mutual respect for state sovereignty'. India became the source of raw material and labour because that suited Britain's germinating industrial ambitions. As H. H. Wilson comments in *History of British India*:[15] 'It was stated in evidence (in a parliamentary enquiry of 1813) that the cotton and silk goods of India could be sold for a profit in the British market at a price from 50 to 60 per cent lower than those fabricated in England. It consequently became necessary to protect the latter by duties of 70 per cent and 80 per cent of their value, or by positive prohibition. Had this not been the case . . . the mills of Paisley and Manchester would have been stopped at their outset, and could scarcely have been set in motion, even by the power of steam. They were created by the sacrifice of Indian manufacture.' It was not, as the school textbooks are apt to suggest, the rise of technology that fired Britain's industrial revolution, so much as the fact that India's wealth enabled us to pay for it.

Of course among the fabric of British rule are threads of conscience and deep concern for the Indian people. But the mythology of India as the white man's burden is new. As Palme Dutt comments in *India Today* (published 1940), 'Where a Wellington, a Burke, a Clive, a Hastings or an Adam Smith spoke frankly and brutally of the facts of tribune, plunder, and spoilation, where even a Salisbury spoke of "bleeding" India, today, when the basis of power is no longer secure, modern official utterance breathes a sickly sweet philanthropy.'

The point of all this is not to beat breasts or thump tubs, but to show that mythology rather than history still influences policy, and is still taken to justify our present ascendancy, the conceit that we have risen to the top on merit, and the belief that it is our natural right to determine the lives of our less fortunate brethren. Mythology, and not historical appraisal, led Lyndon Johnson to proclaim his country as the world's natural leader, and mythology led Unilever's chairman to the boast that 'we are the pace setter for growth and social progress',[16] and to the underlying belief that our present exchange of technology for raw material mirrors the natural relationship of the sophisticated and the backward.

Present trade patterns reflect the imperial past; the egregious imbalance of power between the ruler and the ruled. Thus Third World countries increased their agricultural exports by 2 per cent per year between 1961–63 and 1970–72 – yet the total value of their exports increased by only 3·3 per cent over the whole period. Conversely, Third World food imports – mostly of cereal – also doubled between 1955 and 1966 (although the increase since slowed to around 3·4 per cent per year); but in 1955 the Third World paid 996 million US dollars for their food imports, and an estimated 9,000 to 10,000 million US dollars in 1973–74. Kissinger's suggestion that we all benefit from being linked to the same economic system, rich and poor pulling together, does not stand up. The poor come off badly in their trade with the rich, precisely because the rich are so rich. The inequity is self-perpetuating.

An aspect of the western conceit that the rest of the world needs our succour is the US's claim to be the bread-basket of the world. We can't go on propping up these countries for ever, a US delegate told me at the World Food Conference. Yet as Georg Borgstrom has pointed out,[17] most of the exported produce of the world's greatest agricultural exporter goes not to the hungry world, but to Europe. Three-quarters of the total world grain trade is a flow from the US to Europe, and Europe also buys wheat from River Plate countries and millet from tropical Africa. Only one-tenth of the vast soya acreage in the US is destined for human food, and three-fifths of that exported goes to Western Europe, one-third to Japan, and another 8 per cent is shared between Canada, Israel and Taiwan. England alone gets 12 times as much US wheat per head as India does, and in a couple of years in the 1960s Holland, proud exporter of ham and dairy produce, alone purchased more skim milk to feed livestock than the hungry world received through UNICEF and other aid programmes.

The statistics change constantly, but the pattern does not. The US is not a bread basket, but a table laid for a banquet, from which crumbs occasionally fall. Our justification of our own ascendancy is no stronger than that of the medieval baron, who succoured his serfs, but bled them nonetheless.

Foreign investment, too, may help Third World countries, but not necessarily. One negative aspect was revealed by Salvador Allende, then president of Chile, at the United Nations Conference on Trade and Development in 1972, held in Santiago.[18] Latin America received 3,900 million dollars in foreign investment capital between 1950 and 1967, but paid out 12,800 million in return. As he said: 'Our region paid out four dollars for every dollar it received.' No moral indictment of the businessmen is necessary; only a fool would invest abroad without reasonable returns. But the price for the host is inevitably high.

Second, perhaps more insidiously, a foreign factory may compete with local traditional industries, and will inevitably employ fewer people. A country that plays host to a foreign industry inevitably becomes closer, economically and socially, to the country whose industry it imports. You cannot produce detergent or cars or Coca-cola for foreigners without yourself becoming consumer-orientated. Which again raises the question of whether the west, which makes most of the foreign investments, is providing a suitable model for others to follow.

And here we find the impasse. We have already seen that US and UK style food production is probably not a suitable model for the rest of the world. Our material aspirations in general are too high for others to emulate. More, our civilized trappings – our easy democracy, our freedom of speech – have, historically, depended on a level of affluence far greater than most Third World countries can reasonably hope to achieve; the hiccups in the economy seen in Germany in the 1920s, or in Britain and the US in the 1930s, caused enormous hardship and oppression, yet all those countries, at their lowest ebb, were richer than most of the Third World can foreseeably aspire to be.

More yet, the wealth that underlies our present ease has largely come from the Empires that now make up the Third World. And who will be the Third World's Empire?

In short, if we seriously believe that a well-fed population in a stable world is a worthwhile goal, then we must accept that western development has been a unique and unrepeatable phenomenon; that we are not the world's leaders, as Lyndon Johnson suggested, because we cannot be followed. We must, as I said, re-think. And that is realism.

World Farm
and Self-Sufficiency

If Third World countries cannot hope to buy their way out of trouble by hitching their economies to those of the west – if they both pursue impossible ideals and squander their resources in their attempt to do so – what hope is there?

In the late 1940s China was at least as great a disaster area as India: it had suffered a comparable history of rule by war-lord followed by exploitation by Europe, the US, and Japan. It was poor and hungry and lacked the organization, the *infrastructure*, needed to pull itself out of the mire. Less than 30 years later the Chinese still have problems (which they appreciate more clearly than any foreign sceptic: they admit to political shortcomings and to poverty) but though their numbers have doubled since the revolution, the Chinese do not go hungry. China is a world force which means, above all, that no other country has the power to interfere with it. And China is the only country whose population comes close to straining its physical resources – in contrast to the sparsely populated US, or Canada, or Australia – yet is confident of its ability to ride out natural disaster or foreign disputation. It is at least sensible to ask how China did it.

China began, of course, by analysing her own problems. That the people were numerous and were becoming more so, that they were largely illiterate and had acquired the defensive passiveness that comes from having no control over their own destiny; that the climate was often harsh and always uncertain; that the country had no money for the machines and fertilizers that in the west were seen as the *sine qua non* of productive farming – these were accepted as facts. Also accepted was that the people as a whole were not stupid; that they were used to hard work; and that they had developed techniques of farming and cooking adapted to chronic lack of resource.

Mao Tse Tung was of course a key figure, and part of his genius was his humility. He asked what the people needed, both materially and spiritually, and the Chinese have never stopped asking. He asked what the people could do – 'learn from the people' is one of his key dictums – and set out to build an economy, a blend of agriculture and industry, that was geared to the people's needs, and made use of their abilities. He did not whine about overpopulation, though superficial judgement suggested that China was vastly overpopulated. He did not try to impose the ready made technologies and policies of the west upon the people. To the unbiased observer, one of the most striking features of Chinese politics is not the dogma, but the lack of it: the constant adjustment of outlook and practice in the light of knowledge and changing events.[19] This is in marked contrast to the politics of the west, and to the policies that the west tends to impose on Third World countries, in which the people gear themselves to the logic of capitalism, and to the machines that make capitalism work; in which problems are fitted, or not, into ready-made solutions.

The most obvious single feature of Chinese policy since the revolution has been the desire to become self-reliant. They have not always succeeded: they were hungry at first and have at times imported basic foods since. But agricultural self-reliance has always been and remains a fundamental ambition.

Self-reliance has not been the policy of most western or Third World countries in the past 150 years. Britain quite arbitrarily decides not to grow all her own staple food. Sri-Lanka, then Ceylon, was self-sufficient until her economy became dependent on tea exports: she became self-sufficient again during World War II when the shipping lanes were interrupted; then after the war deliberately eschewed self-reliance in favour of cash-crops.

And whereas Kissinger spoke at the 1974 World Food Conference of 'the inadequacy of the nation-state and the emerging imperative of the global community', China urged national self-reliance as the key both to political independence, and to adequate food supply. 'To depend on food imports is no long-term policy,' said her delegate. And, 'so long as a country works unremittingly in the light of its own specific features and conditions and advances along the road of independence and self-reliance, it is fully capable of solving its food problems.' Even if this proves not to be literally true in all cases, it has already proved true of the biggest and in many ways least tractable Third World country of all.

Kissinger's idea of 'global community' was not simply a piece of rhetoric; neither was he merely saying that all nations must pull together to help each other out. In truth, the idea of treating the whole world as one big farm has greatly influenced national and international agricultural policy throughout this century.[20] The 'world farm' idea has often been corrupted, and used to mask imperialism. But it is also a respectable and sensible notion, which arose for commendable reasons as well as to conceal exploitation. It is worth examining the origins of the idea of world farm precisely because it is a beguiling and still influential concept – and yet is disastrous.

The idea of world farm is partly the logical development of world trade in food; and there is nothing wrong with trade *per se*. Thus in the middle ages – to confine this discussion to the Christian era – Europe imported spices from the east. These served a gastronomic purpose in the days when fruit and vegetable varieties lacked today's versatility, and aided preservation when livestock could not be fed through the winter, nor the carcasses frozen. Marco Polo's overland excursion in the thirteenth century was partly a search for spices: and the maritime explorations of the fifteenth and sixteenth centuries (including Columbus's voyage to America) were undertaken largely to open up spice routes.

But so long as transport was supplied by camel or by the tiny sailing ships of the sixteenth century and before, the food trade had to be confined to products that were non-perishable, of small bulk, and of high value. The fast and relatively large sailing vessels of the seventeenth century opened the way for bulkier and more perishable goods. Imported tea, coffee, and chocolate changed the social habits of an entire class of Europeans during the seventeenth century. And because such goods were bulky, and consumed in much greater quantities than spices, their production needed large plantations. Increasingly these came under the control of the buyers – the Europeans. Direct territorial control, by Europe over Asia, rapidly developed in the eighteenth century.

The fast sailing clippers still operated in the nineteenth century, but the days of sail were numbered. The new steamships, or steam-plus-sail ships, could carry not simply high-price food luxuries, but staples. The first regular and large-scale traffic in cereals – large enough to influence the entire agricultural economy of Britain, for example – had begun, and at the turn of the century to this was added, by the use of chilled vessels, regular trans-world traffic in meat.

The large-scale transport of even the most perishable of commodities was an exciting development. All countries have to accept that some regions are better suited to some crops than to others. Even in a small country like Britain it makes sense to concentrate grain production in the east, which is relatively dry, and to grow grass in the wetter west – and then exchange surpluses between the two. And if you can apply this principle over the whole world – as the growth of world shipping suggested was feasible – why not? The endless plains of Argentina could be used for beef production, to which they are supremely suited: the endless prairies of the US for wheat and corn; the tropics for those high-value, highly desirable cash-crops that only they can produce. In short, all the world's land can be used for what it produces best; and all the world's people can theoretically base their diet on all the world's commodities. The common agricultural policies of the EEC reflect this kind of strategy – Britain asked to concentrate on producing beef, for example, and to leave fruit and vegetable production to the sunnier continent.

So what's wrong?

We have already seen some disadvantages. The economy of countries that are not self-reliant depends heavily upon the economic well-being and good will of those on whom they depend for existence. And trade, to be truly beneficial, must be equitable; yet trade evidently is not conducted equitably when one participant has stronger bargaining power than the other, which is true when rich trades with poor, or when the sale is vital to one side's well-being but not to that of the other. We have seen how the trade works in practice: the steady supply of raw materials from the Third World, with their continued impoverishment; the steady coercion of Third World countries into the ways of the west.

The world farm idea also raises enormous logistic problems, as increasing proportions of the world's shipping, road, and rail – and of the corresponding bureaucracies, of which the Brussels EEC delegates are an example – are concentrated on shifting food. The interruption of shipping in times of war is not in itself sufficient indictment of the world farm idea; it does serve to demonstrate the world farm's vulnerability.

But the world farm idea is unsuited to the needs of the modern world mainly for the reasons outlined in the first chapter: that we must make best use of land. The ideal of the world farm demands that vast areas should be concentrated on producing a single crop – beef, wheat, coffee. The resulting monocultures carry enormous dangers of disease and land-exhaustion, which can only in part be kept at bay by pesticide and fertilizer. More to the point, monoculture does not, usually, produce the maximum amount of human food from a given area. Few areas do not benefit from mixed cultivation – of different crops, of different varieties of the same crop, of crops and livestock, or of crop rotations, either in successive years, or within the same year. This does not mean there should be no extensive arable land or grassland. It does mean, as is universally accepted among agriculturalists, that monoculture has glaring disadvantages and taken overall is profligate. We cannot now afford profligacy, yet monoculture is the stuff of the world farm.

And a large part of our world farm – often the best acres in the neediest countries – is used for cash crops, either for dietary frivolities, such as cocoa, or for animal feed. If the producers of these commodities instead concentrated on producing staples for their own people, then clearly they would have little or nothing to offer the west agriculturally, and the world farm idea would break down. But so long as they do produce these fripperies, then they contribute to the profligacy. If we think we can afford this extravagance, it is because we are insulated from the physical realities. Of course the world farm idea has not been fully realized; but it has helped to shape present policies, and to make the present inequity and profligacy seem respectable. As Kissinger's 'global community' speech showed, it lives on.

At the other end of the scale from the world farm lies national self-sufficiency: no trade, everything supplied from within national boundaries. This idea, in the modern world, makes almost as little sense as the world farm. Almost every country lacks something and is particularly good at producing other things, and it would be merely perverse, unless the country were under siege, not to arrange exchanges. The Chinese said as much at the World Food Conference (see Chapter I).

In short, we are talking about a spectrum: 'global community' or 'world farm' at one end, with every nation acting as a cog in the whole machine; and total self-sufficiency at the other, with each nation standing aloof from the rest. Neither extreme is sensible. But the practical realities of world trade, and the physical realities of a crowded world, make clear that we should pitch our agricultural effort nearer the self-sufficiency end of the spectrum than hitherto. We should indeed strive to become self-reliant, which means producing all we need to get by on, and use trade not as a life-line, but as a way of making life more pleasant. A self-reliant nation is one that produces all the food needed to meet its people's nutritional requirements, but keeps open the option of varying its home-produced basic diet by trade. A self-sufficient nation or community is one that subsists entirely on its own produce. To strive for self-reliance seems highly desirable, since this implies making best use of home agricultural resources. To strive officiously for self-sufficiency – which implies eschewing the benefits of trade – seems unnecessarily extremist.

The idea of national self-reliance has been much mooted in Britain recently – as it has been in many countries in times of economic hardship. Some point out that Britain imports £3,600 million worth of food a year, and that to cut that bill would make Britain richer. That argument is suspect. Britain sustains her prodigious standard of living by trade. She is one of the biggest single importers of US agricultural produce, and agricultural produce is the biggest export commodity of the US. For Britain to pursue a policy of agricultural self-reliance would be to strike her greatest commercial ally (at least until joining the EEC) a powerful blow that would recoil on her with interest. Agricultural self-reliance would not make Britain, or any other western country, richer in cash terms. Britain has opted not to be self-reliant agriculturally precisely because that is the cheaper course.

The west overall – including protein and oil-importing America – would be poorer, if it opted for self-reliance. But national self-reliance in food is the only sensible course open to Third World countries, and if they adopt it then the west must adopt it, if the west believes that the Third World's problems should be taken seriously.

In short, national self-reliance in agriculture for all countries is the only way to solve the world's food problems – which is what this book is about. Those who have mooted self-reliance for Britain have sometimes been dubbed 'little Englanders': and so, unfortunately, many of them are. But those who suggest that Britain's future lies 'in Europe', and with the Common Agricultural Policy of the EEC, might more justly be termed 'little Europeans'. Though it may seem a paradox, we must look inwards in order to take account of the rest of the world's problems.

Of course western countries should not pursue self-reliance precipitately, on a 'cut our imports bill' basis, because the Third World countries do at the moment depend on western trade. But it must become a policy (which at the present time it is not) to be followed in conjunction with the increased self-reliance of Third World countries. Self-reliance will be much harder for some countries than others – extremely difficult for Japan and far harder for Britain and France than for the US. But no country will find it easy, and none, not even the US, can afford to neglect the agronomic and nutritional principles that we must now discuss.

The bones of 'rational agriculture'
What western countries need then, if they are to take the world's food problems seriously, is an agriculture designed to feed their peoples: what I shall call a 'rational' agriculture; that is, one designed

to make best use of the country's own land, while meeting the nutritional needs and gastronomic aspirations of its people.

In cash terms – in terms of today's economics – such an agriculture would be 'uneconomic'. It is commercial lunacy to suggest, as I shall suggest, that middle-sized mixed farms should replace some of today's arable prairies, or that some areas now used for golf courses might be better used for vegetables; if it were not commercial lunacy, then those things would be done already. But I suggest that today's economic norms are based on an inflated evaluation of the worth of western currency – in turn based on the commercial and military dominance that shields the west from the physical realities of an over-exploited world.

But please do not confuse 'uneconomic' with 'inefficient'. 'Efficiency' is an abstract concept – the ratio of inputs and outputs. 'Inputs' in agriculture are a shopping list of many different things – land, fertilizer, labour, building, machines, fuel, feed, and so on. In order to total up the inputs we give each a price. But the prices are based on present commercial realities: labour is dear so we try to make minimum use of it; fuel has been cheap so we have concentrated on machinery. And up till now food could always be bought in from elsewhere, if we found it too expensive to produce at home. But once we begin to see how fragile are our present cash valuations: the extent to which cheap fuel and fertilizer have depended on our military strength relative to the producer countries: how precariously we live if we consciously elect to use good agricultural land for non-agricultural purposes; then we can appreciate how inappropriate our valuation of the relative worth of the various agricultural inputs has been. And the agriculture that is so 'efficient' in today's cash terms may be highly inefficient in terms of making best use of land, or meeting the nutritional needs of the people.

A rational agriculture is not 'inefficient' or 'unrealistic' simply because it may at present seem 'uneconomic'. Rather are today's cash assessments unrealistic since they take little account of the well-being of people outside the western world, and still less of the world's physical limits.

Rational Agriculture

A rational agriculture, leading to national self-reliance, is one that makes best use of the land, while meeting the nation's nutritional needs and gastronomic aspirations. 'Making best use of the land' means producing the most and the best possible human food; but it also means farming conservatively, so that the land is not steadily run down, as tragically is often the case both in the west and the Third World. We must also recognize that farm land is not simply a food factory. Farms should provide many satisfying jobs – as opposed to a few harrowing ones, which increasingly is the case today. The country-side should be a cultural and educational asset for townspeople – and I am not simply talking about the flat and debased concepts of 'leisure' and 'amenity'. I mean that the schism between town and country, the lack of 'feel' among society in general and its leaders in particular for the land and the people who work on it, is one of the chief impedi-ments to agricultural progress, and a major source of nonsense talked about food policy. School children brought up to believe that food is not eatable unless sanctioned by triple wrapping and TV ads; politicians who think a dairy enterprise is mere statistics – rational agriculture lies the other side of that cultural and conceptual desert.

I found it more convenient to talk about land use before discussing nutrition in detail. But I must sketch in a few nutritional premises, so we know what we should be growing.

First, agriculture must provide people with food for energy – and though fat or protein may do so, carbohydrate (particularly starch) is the most conveniently produced energy source.

Second, we need sources of vitamins and minerals.

Third, we need sources of protein and 'essential fat', because these are the stuff of human flesh. Although nutritionists have tended to exaggerate the amount of protein people need, it makes sense to build agricultural strategy around protein production. This is because pro-tein is nutritionally essential; is required regularly, in fairly large amounts; and agriculturally, is one of the hardest things to produce in large amounts. If we can get the protein right, then we will have broken the back of the problem.

Fourth, although meat, eggs, and milk are not nutritionally vital –

even their most critical ingredient, vitamin B_{12}, can be got from micro-organisms and could easily be manufactured in the required amounts – they are nonetheless nutritionally desirable, and gastronomically highly desirable. So within the limits imposed by the need to be self-reliant – and without recourse to the cruelty that mars so much husbandry, traditional and modern – we might reasonably contrive to produce as much meat and other animal products as possible.

Fifth, as with meat, so with green vegetables and other salads and fruit; perhaps they are not nutritionally vital, and certainly not in large amounts, but they do make nutritionally worthier foods more exciting. Fruit is an important source of alcohol, and can be used to flavour grain spirit, as in many European variants of schnapps. Dr Kenneth Blaxter has suggested that the nutrients in barley might be stored most conveniently in the form of beer.[21] I just feel that a diet without greens and onions, fruit and booze would be too sad by half: and again, within the limits of self-reliance, we might reasonably aspire to produce as much as possible.

So much for the requirements. How do we meet them? Protein first: the focus of our effort.

By far the greatest source of protein, world-wide, is green leaves.[22] You may think that statement is a misprint, yet common sense shows the truth of it: the protein in meat ultimately comes from plants, mostly from leaves, and much is wasted in the transition; and the protein in seeds, such as cereals and beans, is made in the leaves – again with much loss in transport within the plant. An acre (0·4 ha) of cabbage may contain almost nine cwt (460 kg) of protein.

But the protein in leaves is contained in the leaf cells which are bounded by cellulose: and leaf protein is extremely diluted, both by that cellulose and by water. Animals that can subsist on leaves have spectacular anatomical adaptations – the rumen of cattle, sheep, camels, giraffes, and deer; the fore-stomach of the kangaroo; the various diversions of gut in the horse and rabbit – that enable them to cope with cellulose in particular and bulk in general. Humans lack these adaptations.

In practice leaves have three applications as a protein source. First where leaves – including grass – grow well and other things do not, as on unimproved wet slopes, they are useful as fodder. Second – as N. W. Pirie has shown – the protein in leaves can be extracted by machine, and used as human food.[23] Pilot schemes, extracting alfalfa protein are already underway in India; and the technique may also be used to convert such weeds as the water hyacinth, which chokes many eastern waterways, into a nutritional asset. I believe that leaf protein as developed by Pirie is the only 'unconventional' protein source (other than unconventional livestock) that may contribute significantly to the world's food problems. (Note that it is for the most part merely an extention of conventional, rational agriculture. Leaf protein production techniques are not designed to side-step agriculture, nor simply to justify the misuse of land for cash-crop plantations.) Third, grass or other leaf protein may be utilized most efficiently if a protein-rich juice is first extracted and fed to pigs, and the residue, perhaps fortified with a non-protein nitrogen source such as urea, fed to cattle. Such a process is already finding commercial application. That does not prove its worth in a rational world, but it shows the idea is practicable.

But our main task is not to find sources of fodder, since to pass nutrients through animals is inevitably wasteful: nor is it to look for unconventional human food sources for the sake of it. We need protein sources suitable as human food without radical conversion. The most productive of such sources is the potato. An acre may yield more than three cwt (150 kg) of protein.

And – though the potato's protein content varies slightly – figures on human protein requirement now supplied by the World Health Organisation and the Food and Agricultural Organisation of the United Nations suggest that the potato alone is an adequate protein source for human adults.[24] Eating potatoes need not make you fat: their protein-energy ratio is roughly what humans need. History has documented the potato's nutritional adequacy time and again. The Irish and West Highlanders of Scotland in the early nineteenth century virtually lived on potatoes and the Irish labourers were renowned for their muscle. They built the English canals and railways that gave the industrial revolution its impetus. The potato, which grows at high altitudes, made possible the civilization of the Andes.[25] Today it also supports Sherpa societies in the Himalayas.

The potato is also a major source of vitamin C – particularly if you leave the skins on: indeed it supplies about a third of the vitamin C in the British diet.[26] This is lost when potatoes are canned or made into 'instant mash' (though the processor may add some to make up) but not when they are equally instantaneously chopped up to make what the English call chips and the Americans, French fries.

Yet the conventional dietician, anxious for his or her charges' health, often declares war first on the chip buttie. Of course if you are poor, and a child, and are obliged to subsist on chip butties, and if the bread in the butties is the modern sliced wrapped, and if the chips are an hour old when eaten, then they make a poor diet. But the chip buttie made with good bread and eaten fresh is a sound basis for an adequate diet, and we would do better to rail against poverty than against the foods that have helped people to survive it.

In an austere world, the potato's nutritional merit and its agricultural and gastronomic versatility make it – literally – a godsend. Every week I read yet another report of a new bean variety, or a new industrial gimmick, that will save the world. Every day the potato is condemned as 'stodge' and breeders are obliged to spend much of their time striving not to increase its merits still further, but for standardization, to placate the manufacturers of potato crisps, to facilitate mechanical harvesting, and to satisfy EEC regulations.

The next most productive protein source is the cereals;[27] an acre can yield about 2·8 cwt (140 kg) of protein. (The figures for protein yield per acre should not be taken too literally: in practice they can vary several fold. They are intended to indicate order of magnitude and demonstrate the relative merits of various protein sources.) In general, as with the potato, cereals alone are an adequate protein source for adults – not too diluted by bulk, nor supplying too many calories per unit of protein.

Oats are the richest cereal protein source, and they are also oily; this is a nutritional bonus, but it makes oats more difficult to store, as they tend to become rancid. History again illustrates their nutritional quality: though Dr Johnson may have considered them fit only for horses, the eighteenth-century Highland Scots did not, and the Duke of Cumberland's soldiers noted that the men they slaughtered at Culloden were sound in limb.

Oats, like rye, are good rough-weather plants; they are gastronimically versatile – used in cakes, porridge, and stuffings – and with a little breeding, could be even more adaptable. But they are now grown mainly for animal feed, and even in Scotland, their traditional home, acreage is fast dwindling.

Wheat is the world's most widely grown cereal, with a protein content that almost certainly could support an adult. Rice is the second most widely grown, though unfortunately with a slightly lower protein content – at least the protein content may not be sufficient to support the prodigious growth of the modern US American; but such spectacular development may not be a good thing, in terms of health or longevity.

Maize, which Americans call corn, is high yielding in sunny climates, and gastronomically desirable. It is the staple in 16 countries in Latin

America and sub-Saharan Africa. Sorghum and millet are crops for dry zones.

The cereals between them span the globe, covering 70 per cent of all cultivated land, and are by far the greatest single source of human food. Adequate fertilization is probably the greatest single worldwide desideratum – and here we should remember that fertilizer applied to poor soils, as in India, has a far greater effect on yield than when applied on the already enriched soils of the west. But some of the few pieces of high science I really do believe in are the attempts to increase soil fertility by trapping atmospheric nitrogen. Scientists in America and Britain – work on corn at the University of Rio de Janeiro seems to be the most advanced[28] – are attempting to produce cereal varieties that carry 'nitrogen fixing' bacteria in their roots, as pulses and some other plants, such as the alder, do naturally. And Professor C. E. Fogg at London University has suggested that blue-green algae, growing on the soil surface, not only supply growing rice with much of its necessary nitrogen, but might, with a little applied science, be induced to supply even more.[29]

But the general point, which should be written in letters two feet high above the bed of everyone interested in the world's food problems, is that a nation that gets its cereal production straight need have no food problems.

And so to the pulses – beans, peas, lentils, chickpeas, and groundnuts. As far as the west is concerned, beans are the chief pulse. The food industry has discovered how to make beans – particularly soya from the US and British field beans (related to broad beans) – into ersatz meat, and has therefore, with the approval of academics, hailed the bean almost as a new discovery; a world-saver. In truth the soya in the east, the broad bean and its relatives in Europe, and the kidney bean's variants in Central and South America have not only helped sustain great civilizations for thousands of years, but have been extolled by all great cooks. They are not fodder that needs to be transmogrified by technology; they have long been the stuff of peasant and grande cuisine.

The yield of beans is notoriously fickle: a three-fold swing from year to year is common with many types. On average, protein yield per acre is similar to that from wheat – say about two cwt (100 kg) – though a good soya crop may easily exceed that. Their protein concentration is generally higher than in cereals – in the case of soya, by several times. An adult relying exclusively on cereal for protein would have little margin for error, but most beans provide easily enough.

Soya is the best bean of those now widely grown, in terms of protein yield per acre, protein concentration, and protein quality. But it
makes no sense, in our design of rational agriculture, to transport
soya from warm climates where it grows well, into colder countries;
nor to strive – as British agriculturalists have done for at least 60
years – to develop soya strains for temperate lands. The traditional
beans of mild and cold climates are perfectly adequate; and as we will
see in the next chapter, the extra protein that soya might supply is
generally nutritionally superfluous. But since soya beans are now one
of America's most valuable exports, the US would have to re-think its
economy radically if the rest of us stopped coveting them.

Beans have other assets, besides their nutritiousness and gastronomic versatility. The plants carry bacteria on their roots that 'fix' atmospheric nitrogen; though in practice beans tend to require heavy
fertilization, they nonetheless may leave the soil as fertile as when
they were planted, or even richer. Also, they are unrelated botanically
to cereal or potato, the other great staples, and in general have
different pests and diseases. Thus beans are a useful 'break' crop –
breaking disease cycles, breaking the steady drain on soil fertility.
Beans' leafy relatives – clover and alfalfa – are similarly used to break
the monotony of grass, the leafy relative of the cereals. In short, a
rational agriculture should produce plenty of beans.

Which leaves livestock. We will see that both the nutritional need
for animal protein and the gastronomic importance of meat have been
grossly exaggerated. In particular, increased meat sales in rich countries have been taken as proof positive of 'public demand' and this
in turn, has been taken to indicate an intrinsic, overweening predilection for meat; and that line of thought is extremely sloppy. But livestock affect every facet of agriculture, and many other aspects of life.
Farm animals play a crucial role in the economy and social life of the
whole world. So we must discuss livestock at length and in several
different contexts. For the moment we will simply discuss the physical
aspects of livestock in the context of rational agriculture.

First, the protein yield per acre even from the most productive livestock enterprises is far below that of beans. Dairy cows may yield
around 0·9 cwt (45 kg) of protein per acre in their milk.[30] If the calves
are raised alongside, to produce a dairy-plus-beef enterprise, the yield
falls to around 0·8 cwt (40 kg) per acre. Broiler chickens can give you
around 0·7 cwt (35 kg) per acre, egg production around 0·6 (30 kg),
pigs about 0·4 (20 kg) and beef and sheep around 0·2 cwt (10 kg) of
protein per acre. Note that these figures are not only rough, as all

such figures must be, but contrived. After all, in the modern world only a few animals actually occupy the fields that feed them; protein yield per acre means the amount of protein an animal produces if given an acre's worth of feed, and that obviously depends, among other things, on the nature of the feed. But the figures illustrate the animals' productivity relative to each other, and to the chief sources of plant protein. In general, livestock production is profligate: in general, cows yield more protein than sheep; and so on.

But we must look deeper. Food animals fall into two main categories. First, there are those that can thrive on leaves (including grass) – which, as we have seen, supply plenty of protein but not in a form suitable for man. This group includes the ruminants – primarily cows, sheep and deer – and the non-ruminants, horses and rabbits.

Secondly, there are the omnivores that can thrive only on food that theoretically could nourish a human being. Chief of these are pigs and poultry.

But it is more useful, in practice, to divide livestock enterprises into those that compete with humans for food, and those that do not. The latter category has two main components. First, cattle, sheep, horses or deer may thrive, or at least get by, on land too steep, cold, hot, wet, dry, salty, or high to be used for more productive purposes. A large proportion of Britain's agricultural land is 'upland', where sheep are a sensible 'crop'. The Icelanders and several groups of British farmers graze sheep on seaweed, or salt-marsh, or what you will. The American bison is already proving its agricultural worth on the US plains which may erode when ploughed. Thus, as Kenneth Blaxter has constantly emphasized, the most rational agricultures have room for livestock, because all countries have ecological niches that only livestock can fill. Vegetarianism is interesting and useful, but overall is not necessary.

One proviso. Rich countries tend to write off land as being fit only for sheep simply because its more productive use would not be profitable. In the nineteenth century the productive subsistence crofts of the Highlands were 'cleared' to make way for sheep that brought the lairds more profit; in the US small high-yielding but 'marginal' farms have often fallen foul of more profitable cattle ranches. The unpromising hills of China, and perhaps even more spectacularly of Japan, are lovingly terraced and nurtured, yielding excellent rice and vegetable crops; the barren hills of Spain, terraced by the Moors, yield olive and grape; a group of exiled Tibetans recently began – to the astonishment of the locals – to grow barley high on the slopes of Wales. The

Tibetans have gone now, but not because their crops failed. In short, though it is dangerous to assume that apparently productive land – such as that of the Amazon basin – would make equally productive agricultural land if cultivated, it is equally dangerous to assume that what is now written off as 'marginal' land is necessarily unproductive. Often such land is written off purely for reasons of accountancy – reasons that may be inappropriate if we accept the need for rational agriculture in an austere world.

The second category of 'non-competitive' animals are those that flourish on food that might theoretically nourish humans, but is aesthetically beyond the pale. Thus pigs traditionally were fed on swill, or on 'chat' potatoes, or apple windfalls or acorns; among some 'primitive' (but highly adapted and impressively disease-free) peoples, pigs and dogs feed on human excrement. Chickens traditionally got by on household scraps, or 'tail-corn'.

The scope for such 'non-competitive' livestock is enormous. Britain and the US allegedly waste 25 per cent of their food after it leaves the farm;[31] about half that is lost after it leaves the plate. The Chinese, cashing in on the obsessive and traditional conservatism of their peasants, allegedly have more hogs per head of population than the US Americans – yet those hogs do not compete with humans for food. This does not mean the Chinese have more pork than the Americans: their pigs are smaller and grow more slowly than the intensively fattened US stock. But it is an impressive yield, on minimal input of resource.

The most obvious example of 'competitive' livestock is that fed on grain, soya, and fish, which are mostly suitable for human food. Britain feeds about two-thirds of its home-grown cereal to pigs and poultry, and to a lesser extent to cattle – though 'barley beef' enjoyed a boom in the late 1950s and 1960s. Half the harvested agricultural land in the US is planted with feed crops: almost four-fifths of all its grain is fed to animals. In all, Americans give their livestock around 20 million tonnes of protein a year in a form that could perfectly well be eaten by human beings. The livestock in turn provide about two million tonnes of protein. The 18 million tonne loss is equivalent to 90 per cent of the yearly world protein deficit: enough to provide everyone in the world with about a quarter of their daily protein requirements.

The Russians are coming up fast, and now feed about a third of their grains to livestock. As we have seen, their massive purchases of grain on the world market in 1972 exacerbated the crisis of that time.

But their consumption is modest compared to the US. Third World countries feed between zero and 10 per cent of their grains to livestock. Grain, of course, is only part of the story: you might add, for example, 95 per cent of the US unexported soya crop.

Such extravagance in a hungry world is ludicrous. But even within the constraints of a rational agriculture, designed to produce food rather than wealth, we cannot simply say 'non-competitive good, competitive bad'. Often we must squander sprats to catch mackerels.

Cows can produce more protein per acre than any other beast. They are the most efficient 'converters' of grass. And grass may often usefully be grown on land that is difficult to cultivate in other ways – as on wetlands, or wet hillsides. Hence cows may be non-competitive.

But dairy farming traditionally requires an enormous labour force. Today, that labour force is largely replaced by machinery, so that a man who before the war might have looked after a dozen cows, may now tend 70 or more. Largely because of the machines, dairy farming has become a high-cost enterprise. It makes no sense – in cash terms – to invest in milking parlours, pasteurizing units, and the rest, and then use low-yielding cows: and it makes no sense to put cows with a potential for high yields on to marginal land. In practice, then, modern dairy units tend to occupy prime land. In practice they may be highly competitive.

Yet all is not so simple. Grass is a useful crop – serving as it does to break the disease cycles of other crops. It also pays from time to time to run livestock on arable land or market gardens. Hence grass 'breaks' – leys – are being reintroduced even into the emphatically arable fields of East Anglia: and this makes sense in rational as well as cash terms. So we may at times rationally use good land for grass, even though this may cause short-term losses in protein production.

Incidentally, the importance of milk in human nutrition has been greatly exaggerated. Nutritionists have rightly observed that milk is a good emergency food for badly nourished people – though not for that enormous proportion of the world's people who cannot digest lactose, the chief sugar in milk, and indeed are made ill by it. But though milk, with its range of vitamins and minerals and its high quality protein, is a good stop-gap for people whose social deprivation causes them to eat badly, it has little relevance for people with access to a proper range of agricultural products. The British Dairy Council in the past 20 years has advertised milk on the basis of its protein content – yet, as N. W. Pirie has pointed out, the protein in milk has at times compared in price with that in smoked salmon.[22] The council has also billed milk as a source of instant energy – 'bridging the energy gap' – yet is a poor source of glucose, which might provide energy quickly, and its chief energy source, saturated fat, provides energy long-term, but is a commodity most westerners could do without. In the early 1970s milk was presented as a source of calcium: so it is, but it is an expensive way to buy chalk. In short, dairy farming has a place in agriculture, and milk a place in diet. But in a rational agriculture its place would be far more modest than now.

To revert to our theme. There are many other examples of feeding livestock 'competitively', but nonetheless rationally. You may not always have enough household scraps to sustain your backyard chickens: it is worth keeping corn in reserve to tide them over. The small loss is more than made up by the saving in nutrient in the scraps. On the grander scale, the hills in Britain often carry far fewer sheep than could be sustained by the summer grazing, because farmers cannot afford to feed large flocks in winter. Again, grain, or high quality hay from good pasture, might usefully be invested in winter to allow better use of summer grass.

Finally, butchers – presumably bowing to the consumers – insist on 'fat' meat: even the lean steak beloved of weight-watchers contains far more fat tucked between the muscle fibres than would the equivalent cut from a wild animal of the same species. A modern beef carcass is one-fifth fat; modern swine is one-quarter fat; and a lamb carcass is about one-third fat. Certainly the genuinely lean meat from, say, wild venison is dry if roasted like beef or pork. But pot roasting, using steam to keep the meat succulent, solves the culinary problems raised by fatlessness.

It takes more feed to put a pound of fat than a pound of muscle on an animal. Hence a large proportion of animal feed merely produces fat. Much of this is trimmed away after slaughter. The rest, secreted among the muscle fibres, does the consumer more harm than good. Yet beasts are not considered saleable unless fattened: a fat animal with nicely rounded contours, is said to be 'finished'. Within reason, the fatter the beast, the higher the butchers grade it.

The obsession with fatness clearly wastes feed. It also perverts the course of animal breeding. Animals that grow quickly – put on lots of valuable muscle – are not necessarily those that fatten easily. Indeed, since animals will fatten only when they have eaten more than they need to develop their skeletons and muscle, the ones that fatten most easily are often the ones that do not naturally pack on enormous amounts of muscle.

Hence the huge European beef breeds – Charolais, Simmental, Chianina, and the rest – that are now being imported into Britain, the US, and elsewhere, will grow rapidly even on modest pasture. But they do not fatten on poor pasture – they cannot eat enough. The good fatteners on poor land are the small breeds, such as the Aberdeen Angus. Clearly we get more protein per acre by producing big lean beasts, than small fat ones. And we have already seen that the role of ruminants in rational agriculture is primarily to feed on poor pastures that are no good for anything else: not to wade through the mountains of high grade feed that are needed to produce a beast that is both big and fat.

To abandon our obsession for well-rounded fatty joints need be no gastronomic hardship – especially if we hung meat properly and did not rush it straight into the cooler – and would be nutritionally beneficial. And it would allow the animal breeders to concentrate on producing beasts that grow big, whatever they were fed on, and were not designed specifically to grow fat. Yield of animal protein per acre could then be increased by perhaps 20 to 50 per cent. The early cattle breeders were apt to select for aesthetic characteristics that we now know have no relevance to the beast's performance: the Hereford's white face is a legacy of this; and the long-horn cattle beloved of the early US cattle ranchers, originally selected largely for its headgear, is now more or less defunct precisely because more useful qualities were neglected. But we might ask whether today's breeders, still hooked on 'finish', are really doing what is needed.

The lean-versus-fat issue is highly relevant to what has become one of the most exciting areas of agricultural expansion – the quest for unconventional species of livestock. In Africa, huge antelope such as the eland and oryx thrive on arid savannah on which native cattle, and more especially imported European breeds, barely stay alive.[32] In the highlands of Scotland, the red deer, which can make do on woody heather, and which uses its speed and resourcefulness to avoid bad weather, may flourish where sheep perish.[33] And Dr. E. R. Orskov[34] has suggested that the horse, already raised for meat on France's Massif Centrale, and even the llama, might prove still more suitable for Scotland than the deer; both are beasts of the open space and supremely adapted to low grade fodder, while deer, given a choice, prefer forest and grow much bigger in the royal parks of Windsor and Richmond than on the glen.

In North America the moose,[35] as massive and meaty as almost any bull, although its lankiness disguises the fact, may thrive in forest

that would give way to tundra – an ecological and aesthetic disaster –
if felled. The bison is already proving its worth as 'livestock', and not
simply as a target for heroic Buffalo-Billery. The musk-ox and reindeer
are supremely adapted to sub-Arctic conditions. The semi-acquatic
capybara, a huge sheep-like rodent, has exciting possibilities as a food
animal in the wetlands of its native South America. The kangaroo,
middle-sized, meaty, almost able to survive without surface water (as
the oryx can) and pernickety in its eating habits, could often usefully
replace or complement the goat, which tends to over-graze and needs
far more water.

But these 'wild' animals, which might sometimes profitably be
ranched, or sometimes merely culled, tend not to put on fat. If we
once began to see leanness as an asset, then the undoubted ecological
advantages of such beasts might be exploited more enthusiastically.
Interest is growing, however; one encouraging sign of enlightenment.

So much for protein. We can sensibly cultivate grains and potatoes
as the chief source, complementing them with beans. And though
a rational agriculture would produce less meat than now – and far less
milk and butter – we could nonetheless justify a fair quota. What there
was would tend to be lean, or at least fatness might become the prerogative of the scavenger pig or duck. But the meat would have plenty
of flavour – not least because flavour partly depends on what the
animal is fed on, and animals filling odd ecological niches have a more
varied diet than those frantically hustled from conception to slaughter.

The next vital desideratum is a source of essential fat. First we
should examine what this is.

Biologists analyse the structure of animal or plant tissue partly by
staining it with special dyes and then looking at it through the micro-
scope. But only some fats – which quite reasonably are termed 'visible'
– are revealed by this technique. The visible animal fats are what most
people mean by 'fat'; they are the 'saturated fats', manifesting as lard,
suet, calves' foot grease, and human flab. Such fats serve as a store
of energy: weight for weight they provide twice as much energy as
protein or carbohydrate. In practice, wild animals accumulate such fat
only under special circumstances: thus pregnant animals, including
humans, lay on fat stores to tide them over the extraordinary physiological strain of lactation; indeed, bottle feeding has been blamed for
obesity in modern mothers, since the accumulated fat is not dissipated
through milk production.[36] Hibernating animals tend to lay on fat in
autumn, and aestivating animals in spring; while animals in cold environments, notably seals and whales, have subcutaneous fat layers

for insulation – and these also help to reduce surface drag and increase swimming efficiency.

In general, though, saturated fat is purely an energy reserve. We who aspire to eat every day do not need such reserves. And since carbohydrate is an adequate and usually more available energy source, humans do not need to eat saturated fat. In practice, a little – and a rational agriculture would produce only a little, as we have seen – does no harm, and may indeed have some physiological merits: some vitamins are fat soluble, for example. A lot, unless you are adapted to a high fat diet, as eskimoes seem to be, is evidently harmful.

But the essential fats are not revealed by simple staining techniques: they are 'invisible'. Chemically, they are termed polyunsaturated which means, though we do not need to discuss chemistry in detail, that their molecules contain fewer hydrogen atoms than do the saturated fats. The polyunsaturated fats do not serve primarily as an energy store: indeed, they are a major component of the membranes that envelop and traverse every body cell. No less than 70 per cent of the nervous system, key to the biological success of mankind, consists of polyunsaturated fat – not least because the highly active nerve cells are richly reticulated by membranes.

To say that a chemical material performs an essential role in the body does not necessarily mean that it has to be supplied in the food. Many essential components can be synthesized in the body. But the unsaturated fats from which the polyunsaturates are made must be supplied in the food. In practice, the body can manufacture all the polyunsaturated fats within its body structure if supplied with two simple types, linoleic acid, which is found in seeds, and linolenic, found particularly in leaves. Bark, twigs, and growing tips evidently contain both kinds in equivalent amounts. The need for sources of unsaturated fat – which, in contrast to the saturated fats, tend to be oily at normal temperatures rather than solid – is reflected in the acres of sunflower, soya, peanut, rape, olive and the rest, the world over. Most oil crops prefer warm climates, though rape flourishes in temperate zones.

No one has thrown more light on man's need for essential unsaturated fats than Michael Crawford, of the Nuffield Research Institute, London. While many have suggested that green leaves are simply a dietary caprice, or at best a fairly inefficient source of mineral and vitamin, he has underlined their possible significance as a source of the essential linolenic acid.[37] In one study in the US, no significant difference was found between the protein content of the diets of middle-class and working-class children; it was concluded that their diet did not influence their social rise. Crawford has pointed out that the middle-class children in the survey ate a far higher proportion of green leaves. It is at least possible, at least worth a passing thought, that the nerves and brains of the middle-class children were indeed better nourished than those of the poor.

Meat is a key source of essential – polyunsaturated – fats. Crawford suggests that the highly developed nervous system of carnivorous animals, and of omnivorous man, has depended largely on their access to this source. Vegetarian animals by contrast tend to be highly muscular but have relatively smaller nervous systems and brains. And of course it is the lean parts of the animal, not the great wodges of suet and lard, nor the 'marbling' in the modern joint, that provide the unsaturated fat. Hence lean animals – which include wild animals – provide proportionally more of the essential fats than do the modern fat domestic livestock. By fattening our livestock we provide ourselves with saturated fat, which may be harmful, and dilute the essential polyunsaturated fat.

The viscera and brains are particularly rich sources of polyunsaturated fat. Crawford points out that lions habitually eat the viscera of their prey, often leaving the muscle to the vultures and jackals. Gourmets too, of course, eat brain, testicle, liver or sweetbread often in preference to the red meat. The steak-house buff, insisting on fillet, rejecting the offals that were once a significant proportion of the butcher's trade, contrives to be more carnivorous than *Tyrannosaurus rex*. His eating habits are almost without precedent in nature.

This nutritional aside strengthens our suggestion made on grounds of economy, that we should raise lean beasts and look for unconventional, often semi-wild, species. And it emphasizes that we should do as our less rich ancestors did, to their gastronomic and nutritional advantage, which was to eat every part of the beast. Today's emphasis on red meat, and the almost total dismissal of offals now seen in many US cities, paradoxically combines profligacy with self-denial.

And so to vegetables. Their importance as a source of essential fats is still controversial. As a source of minerals and vitamins, they might more profitably be replaced by small factories. As sources of gastronomic delight, essential if we are talking about diet, as opposed simply to nourishment, they are vital. We should grow as many as we have room for when basic nutrition has been taken care of.

Three premises. First, a variety of vegetables is preferable to uniformity. Second, of all commodities, none benefits more than vegetables do from being served fresh. And third, since the only undisputed importance of vegetables is gastronomic, we should concentrate on producing flavour. We may note, in passing, that varieties with the subtlest flavour are often those with least storage quality.

Only the market garden, or the old-style labour intensive orchards, can produce a great variety of vegetables and fruit. And those many varieties that are highly desirable, but which cannot withstand the rigours of packaging and the deep freeze, can be delivered in good condition only if those gardens are close to the markets. Note that this particular component of the rational agriculture, the market garden linked to the city is not a plea for austerity, as was our emphasis on grain or bean protein. Gastronomy at a far higher level than we have come to accept is perfectly compatible with the demands of rational agriculture.

A final note about the commodity on which many Third World economies have depended, and which occupies so much European land and Eurocrat's time: sugar. World production has risen from about 1½ million tonnes in 1850 to around 70 million tonnes today. Consumption in the UK, where records have long been kept, has risen from about 4 to 5 pounds (1·8 kg to 2·25 kg) per head per year 200 years ago to an average of 120 pounds (54 kg) today.[38] Some British children evidently get half their calories from it.

But sugar is a nutritional disaster, as we will see in a later chapter. Gastronomically its overuse is vulgar. It is addictive, but it can be avoided, if you don't get hooked on it, as cigarettes can. Its chief role in the kitchen should be as a preservative – a world without jam would be sad – while nutritionally, as we will see, it is a useful complement to meat, and the mediaeval sweet meat sauces, lingering on as duck with orange, sweet and sour, and glazed hams, are worth re-emphasis. But whereas we can reasonably indulge our taste for meat and vegetables as far as rationality permits, we should strive to make as little use as possible of sugar, and aim for a dwindling acreage.

So much for the products of a rational agriculture. A staple of potatoes and cereals, complemented by beans. Modest but significant amounts of lean meat. Plenty of fresh vegetables; and as much alcohol as we can reasonably produce after we have produced the basics.

Such an agriculture, in today's commercial conditions, would be an economic disaster. Yet if you take the world's food problems seriously, it is necessary. In the next chapter we will discuss the organizational and economic aspects of rationality.

The Organization and Economy
of Rational Agriculture

If you talk about the need to organize agriculture centrally, sooner or later somebody mentions Russia. Western observers give the impression that Russian agricultural organization is, above all, rigid: each region concentrating on particular crops, aiming to meet centrally determined production targets; people working on collective farms with their minds more firmly fixed on Moscow than on the day-by-day, yard-by-yard agronomic problems of the land they work. This may or may not be a fair summary of Soviet agriculture; in any case such organization does not provide a suitable basis for rational agriculture.

On the other hand, the phrase 'self-reliance', which is often used synonymously, but wrongly, with 'self-sufficiency', conjures up an image of individuals, or families, or rambling associations of middle-class self-therapists, doing their own thing: the land split into subsistence plots, to be split again as population grows. The 'realists' rightly point out that this arrangement, too, would be disastrous, as it proved to be in Ireland at the beginning of the last century, as it is in much of Africa and Asia today, as it was in the too-enthusiastic years immediately following China's revolution. The simple arithmetical division of land into peasant holdings may be equitable, but it has little to do with rationality. Arithmetic is no substitute for thought.

In Chapter II we saw that all the world could be regarded as a single giant farm; or that each country could aspire to total self-sufficiency; and we concluded that both extremes were absurd. We needed to pitch camp somewhere between the two – to aim at national self-reliance, but with proper regard for other nations' needs and strengths. This kind of idea applies to the units of rational agriculture within nations except that, whereas different nations might reasonably guard their separateness, the various productive units within a nation could more safely accept their interdependence. But we should aspire neither to the national farm, nor to a collection of subsistence holdings. We need wheels within wheels – with, to borrow the Chinese advice to the World Food Conference, deep appreciation of the 'specific features and conditions' of each country: whether that country be the US, Britain, Germany, Malawi, or anywhere else.

Our shopping list of desirable crops, outlined in Chapter III, largely determines the shape of agriculture. Thus the central task is to grow cereals, potatoes, and beans. These crops need well-cultivated land, and they can reasonably be harvested by machine. We should not say – as tends to be supposed at present – that the bigger the machine the better; but it is reasonable, for example, to do the bulk of the work with 30 or 60 horsepower tractors, rather than 10 horsepower mini-tractors, or horses; and to use combine harvesters. Machines require reasonably flat land (overturning tractors were the main cause of fatalities in British agriculture before safety cabs became compulsory) and room to turn round in. The prairie, in most situations, is an ecologically precarious and profligate use of land; but for mass cereal growing, it is at least reasonable to keep the fields reasonably big. In a rational world, the best, most fertile and most easily cultivated land, would be used for cereals, beans, and potatoes – these in turn being grown as human food, rather than animal feed.

Again, we must accept that different regions, even in small countries, have different strengths and weaknesses. Hence Britain's east side has a drier climate than the west, and has become the traditional centre of cereal growing; the southern states of the US have concentrated more and more, in recent years, on soya production. Both crops are desirable, in their own countries; and regional concentration makes sense.

But rationality tends to end where commerce takes over. To say a general tendency or trend makes sense is not to justify the supreme specialization that is so much a feature of modern farming. At least since introduction of the Norfolk four-course rotation in the eighteenth century farmers have known that to grow the same crop year after year is, in general, bad farming. It robs the soil, and it allows diseases to build up. Ten years' or more uninterrupted barley growing in East Anglia, for example, is made possible only by massive infusions of fertilizer, pesticide and herbicide. This makes commercial sense if barley happens to command a high price, and the chemicals happen to be cheap. It makes less commercial sense in the post-OPEC days when the chemical inputs are expensive. It has always been bad farming practice – mining, not husbanding, the soil.

In general, farms that do not depend on massive injections of chemistry, whose soil is improved with the years, and which, in the long run, are most productive, are mixed farms. And 'mixed' implies a range of crops, the strategic use of livestock, and a variety of each kind of crop, since different varieties have different susceptibilities to disease. Hence a rational agriculture would have its arable regions and its bean and potato regions, but this would be merely emphasis, not exclusive specialization.

Again, every region had its micro-climates. Sassenachs tend to think Scotland is wild and woolly; but parts of its west coast, warmed by the Gulf Stream, enjoy a summer climate that is almost Mediterranean. Every hill in every country has a lee-side, sometimes a dangerous frost-pocket, sometimes (especially if terraced) ideal market-garden territory. The wine-growers, of course, are very aware of the difference in crop quality that a slight slope, or a minor change in soil depth, may make. A rational agriculture, making best use of land, does not overlook micro-climates. It does not write off a hill simply because it is high, or run the plough down a slope that could grow peaches or grapes – for which, as we have seen, a rational agriculture should make room. We can use the micro-climates only by farming on a yard-by-yard basis. That means employing many people on the land. The pride that both Britain and the US take in having reduced their agricultural force four-fold since World War II is inappropriate. It is a tribute only to their commercial strength that they can be so complacently profligate. They use their wealth to compensate for bad farming.

Livestock should of course be fed non-competitively, although, as we have seen, judicious use of feed grains may sometimes allow more thorough exploitation of swill or of summer grazing; and the best-worked land benefits from the odd year under grass, with its attendant sheep and cattle. As we have seen, the grass 'ley' is already creeping back even into today's ultra-specialized arable farms. We may note, however, that today's farmers introduce specialist beef, dairy, or – rarely – sheep enterprises to exploit grass. If we wanted to make best use of the land, with minimum recourse to the veterinary surgeon, we should generally adopt patterns of mixed grazing – since different species favour grass in different stages of growth, and, in general, suffer from different parasites. A 'rational' pattern of grazing, based on ecological principles, might bear only passing resemblance to to-day's uniform, monocultural flocks and herds.

The disadvantages of feeding swill and other scraps to livestock – essential if we are to mop up the 25 per cent of food that we now waste – have received so much emphasis that non-competitive feeding of pigs and poultry is dying a death. Swill feeding is actively discouraged in the US.[39] After all, the household scraps that would make up the bulk of pigfeed need to be collected before they go rotten, and separated from other rubbish. Swill can be, and often has been, a source of animal disease: the swine vesicular disease epidemic in Britain in the early 1970s – at first thought to be foot and mouth disease – began with swill that had not been properly sterilized. And swill-fed pigs and poultry, or those left to scavenge in orchards or stubble, do not grow as uniformly or quickly as those fed a diet scientifically designed to give maximum production.

To make effective use of waste food, we would need to position the piggeries and poultry units close to human habitation – in the towns or on the outskirts – and to employ a lot of people, and subtle techniques of husbandry. In addition, swill-feeding requires a high degree of public co-operation. People must be aware of the need to raise animals in this way, must save and separate scraps, and tolerate the smells and sounds of livestock units. This requires something more than 'public education'; it involves a sense of involvement among all the people in the business of food production.

That should not be too much to ask. The reward of a rational food policy is that life can go on, with fulfilment for each individual. The price of failure is mass death, and that price is already being exacted. Clearly, though, the task of feeding pigs and poultry non-competitively is not feasible if we adopt today's commercial criteria or the aspirations of urban politicians and businessmen – to be forever insulated from the vulgarities of food production.

We already see, however, that different crops require different scales of organization. It makes sense to think big when organizing arable farming – even though each individual arable farm should merely emphasize grain production, and not be wholly committed to it. But when talking of non-competitive pigs and poultry, we think on a smaller scale, since these should be linked to the human habitations that are their chief source of feed. So too with vegetables. We have said we need market gardens, rather than uniform swards of green in which flavour and subtlety is sacrificed to the demands of machine-harvesting and processing. These gardens should be linked to the people they serve – perhaps, as is common in modern China, occupying the suburbs.

Thus, a rational agriculture is organized on a wheels within wheels basis. For some commodities – notably pigs, poultry, and vegetables – each community is more or less self-sufficient. Other commodities, in particular the staples of grain, potato, and bean, and also hill sheep and perhaps unconventional species raised on non-agricultural land, would tend to be grown more regionally.

And although individual self-sufficiency cannot provide the basis for a rational agriculture, nonetheless the idea of self-reliance, the involvement of everybody in the business of food production, the general acceptance that as many people as possible should grow vegetables and raise chickens – this idea is a vital component of rational agriculture: it is indeed the raw material of rational agriculture. Nonetheless each quasi-self reliant community must, if resources are to be used to their best advantage, be integrated in larger and larger units, of which the largest is the whole self-reliant nation. That is what I mean by central organization: not the rigid divisions and collectives allegedly characteristic of Soviet agriculture.

Some general points. I have suggested that everyone should be 'involved' with food production, which in part means growing some of one's own food. But I do not mean that everyone should aspire to be a peasant, or that agriculture should be left to amateurs. The market garden, and not the backyard, should be the chief source of vegetables; and that should remain the domain of the professionals, as should the urban or suburban piggeries and poultry units.

A rational agriculture tends to break down the rigid demarcation between town and country. Towns, concentrations of activity, remain desirable; so too are the wild places. But the suburb, for example, should not be thought of simply as a dormitory as it is now. It should be a productive entity – both tending to self-reliance, and providing some surplus for the more committed town-dwellers. The research from Wye College in Kent (quoted in Chapter I) suggests that such entities could be highly productive.

But however productively you may manage the land without labour, you can produce more with human hands to help. A rational agriculture requires a large labour force. This means fewer people in industries that in today's world yield more cash. This is one of several reasons – we have indicated others – why a country with a rational agriculture would have less spare money than one that expropriates the fruits of others' agriculture. But I suggest that good jobs on the land should bring more human satisfaction than many of today's factory jobs: that the flight of labour from the land since the war had more to do with the social deprivation of country people than with an aversion to farming.

In addition, the most consistent complaint of farmers' unions the world over is not that farmers cannot make an easy fortune, but that farming has been extremely insecure. Britain illustrates this better than most. In times of peace during the past 150 years successive governments have occasionally been tempted to think that farming in Britain was a waste of time: imported food, skimmed from US or Australian surplus or coerced from the Third World was so much cheaper. British farming was commensurately run down.

During the two World Wars Britain had to attempt to become self-reliant: its efforts during World War II both illustrate that such a thing is possible, and show how badly the thing is done if the necessary infrastructure has not been established. Since World War II the vagaries of trade, the rise and fall of the barley boom, the growth of the processors of pig and chicken meat, of frozen peas and bottled blackcurrant juice, have compelled farmers – and compel is the right word – to leap from one band-wagon to the next. Some have made fortunes; many have gone broke. But few have enjoyed the sense of security that is essential both to good farming and to peace of mind: the knowledge that time and money invested in an enterprise this year will be relevant to conditions a few years hence, when the enterprise is beginning to be productive. East Anglian farmers in particular have leapt from enterprise to enterprise with unsurpassed agility since the Second World War: yet it is a fundamental dictum of farming that no worthwhile enterprise can be established in less than a few years.

Here we find one of capitalism's ironies. Individual freedom is held to be one of the ultimate desiderata of human existence. Farmers in particular not only place great store by that freedom, but also require it: only a good farmer knows how his land can be used to best advantage, and that fact alone is a major indictment of agriculture based on central directive. And the spirit of commercial free-for-all that underlies agricultural economies in the west is held to be an essential component of personal freedom. Yet the history of western farming in the past 150 years is one of compulsion. The modern farmer often finds he has to raise pigs, or go broke: having decided to raise them, he has to keep a particular strain, to feed it on a particular mix, to kill the stock at a particular weight and age, or his profit margins go all to pot. He neither enjoys freedom to farm in the way he knows is best for his land, nor does he enjoy financial security – as the notorious swings in the fortunes of pig enterprises illustrate.

Working within the constraints of rational agriculture a farmer would still be impelled to concentrate on particular crops: but the crops would be determined primarily by the nature of his land, and to suggest that bowing to nature is a sacrifice of personal freedom seems merely perverse. And he would be obliged to be productive – but what farmer does not want to be?

Within those constraints the farmer would be free to work as he thought best – since we should recognize that he, albeit with some outside advice and help, knows best how to work his land. Above all, he would be working within the context of a clear agricultural strategy – a strategy designed to provide good food for his countrymen. In short, a farmer would enjoy far greater freedom and security – and security is an important part of freedom – than he now does within the context of free enterprise.

Finally, we must, of course, gear our distribution system and our 'retail outlets' to the rational agriculture, just as the modern supermarket is geared to the present agriculture and food processing. I imagine that the constant flood of fresh vegetables and eggs from the suburbs would most conveniently be channelled into the street markets, market halls and corner shops of past ages. After all the packaging and prolonged shelf-life on which our present centralized food production and retail depend would both be reduced to a minimum. We should not be talked out of rationality by the argument, undeniable though it is, that modern food companies geared to centralization and storage technology could not make a profit out of it.

Economic framework

I have already intimated that many facets of rational agriculture are not profitable – sufficient justification, in some people's minds, to reject the ideas as 'unrealistic'. Yet if we accept that we need rational agriculture in a world that can no longer afford profligacy, then we should not throw it out because it does not fit in with our economy. Rather we should ask what economic framework would be appropriate. After all, the one certain fact about our own capitalist economy is that it developed in a period when the outstanding features of the present world – the impending lack of resource and the world-wide aspiration to national self-determination – did not pertain. We should not be over-surprised if an economy that developed in an earlier age does not prove appropriate to our own.

But we cannot assume that the system of rational agriculture we have described is necessarily characteristic of any particular political system that now prevails. Clearly the system is similar in many respects to that of China: and we can demonstrate that the neatest economic framework to contain the system would be Marxist. Yet it would be nonsensical to suggest that the system is necessarily 'communist': or if it were communist, that it would necessarily be a carbon copy of the agriculture of any existing communist country. Indeed, since the organization of agriculture in China differs significantly from that of the USSR, and since both are considered by westerners to be 'communist', we cannot say that any existing agriculture is characteristic of communist states.

More specifically, the arrangement of overlapping and interlocking farms, market gardens, and smallholdings that I have described could be contained within several distinct political frameworks. All land could be owned by the state, and the farmers paid a salary. Or land could be state-owned and leased to farmers on a sub-contractor basis. Or land could be owned on a local community, or regional, basis. The various possible systems of tenure and payment are not all typical of a Marxist economy: the sub-contractor idea is not at all typical. It is similar to the system whereby doctors are employed in Britain's National Health Service, which is a product of social democracy. A Marxist economy – which does not imply imitation of Russia or China – probably would provide the most satisfactory framework for rational agriculture. But if you want rational agriculture without changing the political habits of a lifetime, you may feel comforted that social democracy could achieve the desired ends.

But it is difficult to see how a rational agriculture could be run on simplistic capitalist lines, as can be illustrated by reference to meat production. Meat has played an important part in human nutrition, and a key role in gastronomy. Yet the emphasis on meat production in the west, which has increased dramatically since the Second World War, has little or nothing to do with either. It is simply a commercial imperative in a capitalist economy.

The fundamental difference between human demand for food, and demand for any other commodity, is that the demand for food is restricted by people's physical capacity to eat.[40] A car manufacturer can gear his output precisely to the buying power of the society in which he sells. If the people are relatively poor, he can supply them with Model Ts. As they grow richer, he can give them Mustangs. Richer still, and he can suggest that one car per family is not enough, or that it is infra-dig to run a car more than six months old; or that a six-litre engine gives a smoother ride than a three-litre one, or that leather upholstery is better than PVC. People's ability to 'consume' cars is theoretically unlimited. The richer they become, the more they can spend on motoring; the more, both in absolute and relative terms, can the car manufacturer take off them.

The farmer cannot 'expand' in the same way. If he grows wealthy, invests more in production, produces more, he finds himself trying to sell five sacks of corn to people who are physiologically capable of consuming only one. Over-production has always been a bane of farmers, and particularly of western farmers since the war. Where old-time farmers prayed for bad harvests, modern western governments prop up their overproductive farmers by taking land out of production, burning or dumping surpluses, introducing support buying, and all the rest. All these devices are designed in part to resolve the paradox that demand for food is 'inelastic', and so the farmer cannot take his share of the increasing wealth of his countrymen.

Livestock provide the buffer, the sump, to mop up surplus. Instead of trying to sell five sacks of corn to people who only want one, the farmer feeds four-and-a-half to pigs, and sells less corn than before, but with meat as well. And if people have a surfeit even of meat, he can begin to throw some of the carcass away: the offals and heads, once prized, find their way into pet-food. Thus, through the agency of meat, agriculture can expand indefinitely. The stifling spectre of 'inelastic' demand is laid.

Similar considerations apply to tea, coffee, cocoa, or fruit production. People's ability to consume such products is for practical purposes virtually unlimited. Fruit, after all, especially in the form of grapes, can be turned into alcohol. But it is meat production, demanding roughly a ten-fold loss in the human food available from a given area of land, that most spectacularly solves the paradox that production must increase if agricultural wealth is to keep pace with the rest of society: yet is theoretically constrained by people's ability to consume. In short, production of non-nutritious cash-crops, but particularly production of meat – as much as possible – is vital to ensure the 'viability' of agriculture in a capitalist economy. Yet, as we have seen, the world as a whole cannot afford the profligacy on which such emphatic meat and cash-crop production depends.

The only appropriate framework in which a rational agriculture can operate is one geared to the recognition that inputs must be used as sparingly as possible, and in which the lack of elasticity of demand is not simply accepted, but positively encouraged. That is not a capitalist framework; and no amount of contortion or coercion can push rational agriculture into such a framework.

Of course western agricultures are not run on strictly capitalist lines; market forces are severely modified – at some times more severely than at others – by tariff, support buying, subsidy, and the rest. And, of course, you could design an agriculture that was designed on capitalist lines, with only the most profitable enterprises allowed to flourish. The trouble is that such an agriculture – which inevitably would be based largely on monoculture, and would inevitably concentrate on high-value commodities such as pork chops and oranges – would not feed the people, and certainly would not be rational, in the sense of making best use of the land. As people grew hungry, the price of staples would increase, and make their production profitable; but an agriculture founded on prices forced high by incipient starvation is hardly satisfactory, and the inevitable swings from enterprise to enterprise as farmers attempted to cash in on whatever happened to be profitable would be bad both for their peace of mind and for the land.

Much of the enormous complexity of western agricultural policies, in particular the Gordian knot of the EEC Common Agricultural Policy, springs from the heroic but foredoomed attempt to squeeze agriculture into a capitalist economy; to reconcile irreconcilables, to extend the analogy between farming and the manufacturing industries, whose productivity is far more readily geared to society's buying power. The complexity, the immense 'difficulties' thus created, are responsible for much of the pessimism expressed by western politicians. And this pessimism in turn is largely responsible for the western liberals' search for morally neutral scapegoats – such as 'overpopulation' – to explain why the world's people are not, nor seem likely to be, well fed.

I do not intend to oversimplify. I do not suggest that the introduction of Marxist economy, or socialist philosophy, will automatically solve the world's food problems. I do suggest that we cannot hope to solve those problems unless we first devise a suitable economic framework for our own agriculture; and that we cannot do that, unless we clearly see the fundamental paradox of our present framework.

Would Rational Agriculture Nourish Us?

Rational agriculture would offer us cereals, potatoes, and beans as our chief sources of protein, tricked out with only modest amounts of meat, milk and eggs. We catered specifically for our essential fat, vitamin, and mineral requirements in designing the agriculture, and the starch of the potatoes and cereals is an adequate source of energy. But have we not sold ourselves short in protein? Are the plant proteins garnished by meat, really adequate?

Let's answer that last question with a categorical piece of provocation: that of all the disasters caused by the mis-application of science in this century, including the development of the atom bomb, none has caused more human misery, or a greater misuse of resources, or a more pernicious perversion of policy and action, than the nutritionists' exaggeration of protein requirements.

At the mundane level, the pre-match beefsteak of football teams is merely ludicrous; perhaps, even, the mythological connotations of meat-eating outweigh its nutritional inappropriateness. More serious are the advertisements urging mothers, who wish to do the best by their children, to buy extra-high protein baby foods that perhaps lead to over-growth – 'hypertrophy' – and launch the infant into a lifetime of incipient obesity.[36] Tragic are the attempts by Third World mothers who waste half their incomes trying to nourish their infants on such foods, while their breasts dry up and the produce of the surrounding fields – which could help the mothers in lactation – is channelled into European piggeries. Largely irrelevant are the attempts of the food industry, backed by governments and lauded by academics, to produce high-protein foods from oil, plantation wastes, or what you will. Destructive has been the apparently altruistic 'dumping' of US dairy surpluses in Third World countries after World War II: these contributed little to nutrition, and helped undermine the native agricultures that are now recognized as the world's prime desideratum.

And utterly stultifying is the pessimism that springs from the belief that people need massive infusions of protein – the belief that wheat is not food, but only raw material for meat production. Even Georg Borgstrom, a prophet of our age, whose *Too Many* and *Hungry Planet* deserve to be read and re-read, fell foul of the protein myth. Writing in the 1960s, when the myth was at its height, he managed to conclude that most of the world is already overpopulated, that we are already living on borrowed time; a conclusion based on the idea that people need a lot of protein, and the observation that of all essential nutrients, protein production requires greatest input of agricultural resource. The resulting sense of hopelessness kills useful action: seems to justify the attitude that since we are all doomed anyway, we might as well enjoy ourselves while we may.

The protein myth – the idea that the world's prime food problem is a 'protein gap' – was founded, as the most dangerous ideas often are, on good intention, sound observation, and eminently sensible reasoning. Donald S. McLaren, of the American University of Beirut, has traced the myth's origins in *The Lancet*.[41] He points out that malnutrition was widely studied in the 1920s and 1930s – and that it presented a confusing picture: because malnutrition is complex, and because at that time the science of nutrition was noticeably more primitive than now.

To give shape to the confusing picture the scientists sought – as they must always do – to quantify. Among other things, this meant measuring each item of the diet, and trying to assess just how much of each was lacking. They also needed to recognize malnutrition more clearly; poor diets can cause anything from thinness (which may, after all, be 'normal' and even aesthetically attractive), or sluggishness (which can have a hundred other causes), or vague puffiness, or increased susceptibility to infection; it is extraordinarily difficult to tell, faced with a thin, sick child, whether he is thin purely for genetic reasons, or made thin by his infection, or whether infection and thinness both have a common basis in poor diet – and if the latter is true why his particular diet is deficient.

A breakthrough – an overused word, but appropriate here – came in 1932, when Cicely Williams, the first woman medical officer appointed to the Gold Coast (now Ghana), described a 'deficiency disease of infants' in which, she said, 'some amino acids or protein deficiency cannot be excluded'. The deficiency disease had clearly recognizable signs: drying of hair and skin; reddening of hair; and a pot belly caused not by obesity but by oedema. Biochemists later demonstrated distinct alterations in blood chemistry – thus giving laboratory confirmation of the more subjective clinical findings.

Kwashiorkor does exist: it is important, particularly in Africa; and though the mechanism is uncertain it does seem to be associated with

C

lack of available protein. Its recognition was a great advance. But fate took over. As McLaren recalls: 'During the late 1930s and 1940s, when international meetings were virtually non-existent and travel was limited, discussion of the nature of undernutrition in children was carried on through the correspondence columns of journals.' Significantly, this correspondence was 'mainly between workers in different parts of Africa', where many people rely on the starchy root cassava, the only one of the world's major staple foods that really is deficient in protein.

Then came World War II. Research was interrupted. When it was over, the newly created World Health Organisation and the Food and Agricultural Organisation of the United Nations were anxious, in a new and optimistic world, to get on with the task of feeding the world's hungry. They built on pre-war observations – all that was available. In 1953, in an influential report entitled *Kwashiorkor in Africa*, they made the much-quoted statement that kwashiorkor was 'the most serious and widespread nutritional disorder known to medical and nutritional science'. This statement, says McLaren, was made 'without reference to the rest of the world and other forms of malnutrition'. But the idea had been firmly planted that protein deficiency was the key to malnutrition.

So far, we have been talking about sound scientific observation pushed a little off the rails by misfortune: the misfortune that the seminal observations sprung from atypical Africa, and that the war interrupted study. But in the 1950s protein production became a bandwagon: the boundaries between altruism and self-interest, between policy based on science or on expediency, became blurred. Thus did the US unload dairy surpluses in Third World countries. And as the surpluses dried up, as they had by 1964, they were replaced by the potentially profitable 'protein rich food mixtures', whose manufacture and distribution was widely acknowledged as necessary succour for the Third World.

McLaren was among those who from the early 1950s doubted whether the extreme emphasis on protein production was justified. And at the International Congress of Nutrition in Hamburg in 1966 he 'challenged the philosophy behind the development of protein-rich food mixtures'. But this 'immediately brought public rejoinders from "the establishment" defending the party line', although 'in private I was told by many delegates that they agreed but were afraid to say so aloud for fear of having their support cut off. Several attempts by me to have the matter discussed at a policy-making level were thwarted and conclusions reached along these lines by delegates to one seminar were actually deleted from the report by the secretariat.'

In truth, although much of today's food policy is either a direct enactment of the protein myth, or is a legacy of it – and the western emphasis on meat, and particularly dairy production, has sometimes been justified in part on nutritional grounds – leading agriculturalists and nutritionists in the United Nations, in the British Ministry of Overseas Development, and many independent clinicians and scientists interested in the Third World have now accepted that protein production has been over-emphasized, and that malnutrition – even kwashiorkor – rarely results simply from lack of protein in the diet.

One of the crucial flaws in the simple idea that malnutrition even 'protein-deficient' malnutrition, necessarily results from lack of protein in the diet, is that it overlooked the concept of protein sparing. A key figure in the development and acceptance of the protein sparing idea is Professor P. V. Sukhatme.

Sukhatme[42] found that malnourished, ostensibly protein-deficient children in the village of his native India improved not only when given protein-rich foods, but also when given more 'ordinary' local foods, such as cereal or beans. Note that such foods are not purely energy foods, as sugar is. They are also sources of protein. But they are not 'high protein' foods of the kind once considered necessary.

Briefly, the children were not short of protein in particular, but of food in general. More specifically, the body needs both energy, to keep it going, and protein, from which to construct and re-construct. But it has priorities: if the body is short of energy, it will first of all metabolize ('burn') the carbohydrate (glycogen) in its muscles and liver; with that running low, it begins to metabolize spare fat; and then, if it is still short of energy, it burns protein. If you give protein to a child who has inadequate supplies of other energy foods, his body burns the protein. Thus he suffers protein deficiency, and may (though not necessarily) begin to show the specific signs of kwashiorkor. Conversely, energy foods will 'spare' his protein and often render the limited supply adequate.

In general, adequate protein nutrition has two separate aspects. First, the body must receive a basic absolute quantity of protein which should be eaten every day, because the body does not store surplus, and any day the body misses out it must draw on the muscle tissue to make up.

Second, the body must be supplied with protein and energy foods in a proper ratio. Give too little energy, and some of the protein will be burnt to make good the energy lack – so even if you give the correct amount in absolute terms, the body will suffer deficiency. On the other hand, give adequate protein and excess energy, and the body will tend to grow fat. Hence you could possibly get enough protein by eating even a low-protein food such as cassava, but you would need to eat so much that you would exceed your daily energy requirements several times over, and finish up spherical.

Anyway, largely as a result of the more subtle appreciation of protein requirements fostered by McLaren, Sukhatme, and others, leading nutritional authorities have reduced the recommended daily requirement of protein about three-fold since 1948: indeed, current recommendations are roughly what they were at the beginning of this century. The absolute figures are less interesting than their practical consequences, but for the record, the National Research Council of America (NRCA) in 1948 recommended that children aged one year should receive 3·3 grams of protein per kilogram body weight per day. By 1957 the Food and Agriculture Organisation of the United Nations (FAO) recommended 2·0 grams per kilogram per day for one-year-olds. In 1971 they brought the figure down to 1·2 grams per kilogram. Adults evidently require only half as much protein (per unit body weight) as growing children.

But though recommended protein requirements have been brought down, recommended daily calorie intake – which in practice is easier to assess – has remained steady: NRCA recommended 100 kilocalories per kilogram body weight for one-year-olds in 1948, while in 1971 FAO were recommending 105 Kcal per kilogram.

Thus the recommended ratio of protein to energy has gone down. According to the 1948 figures, a child would need 15 per cent of his diet in the form of protein. According to the 1971 figures, 5 to 6·5 per cent energy/protein ratio is adequate.

The consequences of this change of mind are profound. For even when you make suitable adjustment for protein quality – a topic we will discuss in a minute – all the world's great staples, and especially the potato, millet, and wheat, are now seen to be adequate protein sources. [24], [27]. If you eat enough of them to satisfy your daily energy requirements – which after all is what staples are supposed to do – then you will automatically satisfy your protein requirements as well. You do not need to eat excessive, fat-making quantities to satisfy your protein needs.

Thus, in the high days of the protein myth, it seemed that people's protein requirements could be met only by supplying large amounts of high-protein foods – notably meat, and perhaps soya. Countries without the reserve capacity to produce a lot of meat seemed to be in a bad way. Now we see – to revert to the comment made in passing in Chapter III – that a country that can grow enough grain to meet energy needs should have no protein problems. Suddenly the world's food crisis seems a lot more tractable.

But we have seen that even austere agriculture should produce some meat. And meat is useful as a protein source, not to provide the bulk but simply to act as a long-stop to the staples. In short, nutritional requirements fit rational agriculture like a hand in a glove.

One further point about protein balance. The main products of rational agriculture – potatoes, beans, and grains – provide protein at the same time as they supply energy. Sugar, the purified white or brown granules of sucrose from cane or beet, does not. Sugar consumption has grown so rapidly in the west in the past 150 years that, according to Professor John Yudkin, the average Britisher now gets about one-fifth of his calorie requirements from it.[38] It infiltrates the diet not merely via tea and coffee, or even, more cryptically, in confections; the food industry uses massive quantities to bulk out ostensibly savoury soups and the like.

But if we take in calories without protein, then it becomes more difficult to maintain a proper protein-energy ratio. Either we get fat by taking in protein-free calories – which indeed westerners commonly do – or else we must increase the proportion of protein in the rest of the diet. If you eat sugar, then you cannot bring your protein-energy ratio to the required 5 per cent simply by eating cereal. You are obliged – if you want to avoid obesity – to resort to high-protein foods to meet the required ratio. Hence high-protein foods are more nutritionally necessary in sugar-eating societies than in those poor or 'underdeveloped' societies that do not eat sugar. If meat is ever nutritionally necessary, it is largely because of the need to counterbalance the protein-free sugar intake. Paradoxically it is the sugar-soaked west, and not the sugarless Third World, that 'needs' meat. This argument may appear to conflict with the 'protein sparing' idea mentioned in connection with Sukhatme. Note, however, that in the studies cited by Sukhatme the children's diet was not supplemented with sucrose, but with wheat and beans which themselves have a proper protein balance.

A word about protein quality. Old-fashioned but still extant nutritional texts emphasized the distinction between 'first-class' and 'second-class' protein, and tend to suggest that animal proteins are first-class, plant proteins second. The distinction makes some sense but, stated baldly, is erroneous. In general, all the body proteins are constructed from sub-units, termed amino acids. Though the body contains thousands of different proteins varying greatly in form and function – enzymes, hair, and haemoglobin, or at least the globin bit, are proteins – all are constructed from only 20 different amino acids.

The body gets its amino acids, from which to make protein, from food. When you eat protein, the gut first breaks it down into amino acids, then absorbs the amino acids, then rearranges them into the proteins it needs.

The body can manufacture most of the amino acids it needs from others. For example, one of the amino acids commonly occurring in body proteins is glycine: but the body does not need a supply of glycine in its food. It can make glycine from any other amino acid you care to supply it with.　But it cannot make all the amino acids it needs in this way. Those it cannot make for itself – there are eight in all – must be supplied ready-made in the food. These are termed the essential amino acids.

An ideal food protein obviously must contain all the amino acids. But more than that: it should contain all of them in the correct ratio. For example, for the body to make haemoglobin, it must have adequate supplies of both lysine and methionine – both of which must be supplied ready made in the diet. If you give the body loads of lysine, but no methionine, it cannot make haemoglobin. If you give a little methionine, then it can make a little haemoglobin – but a large proportion of the lysine would be left over. And since the body cannot store surplus amino acids, the left-over lysine would be wasted. In short, the extent to which the body can utilize lysine depends on the amount of methionine given at same time. This is a highly simplified example: but in general, the value of a given dietary protein depends mainly on whether it contains the essential amino acids in the correct ratio. If it is a bit short of any one, then a corresponding proportion of the others will be wasted.

So-called 'first-class' proteins do contain all the essential amino acids in roughly the ratio required by the body. Hence the body can make good use of almost all the protein contained in, for example, egg. So-called 'second-class' proteins are a bit short of one or other of the essential amino acids. The most notorious shortfall is in cereal proteins, which tend to lack lysine.

There are four big 'buts' which render this simple conventional analysis, accurate though it is in essence, both misleading and largely irrelevant. First, the distinction between first- and second-class proteins is not absolute. The proteins found in conventional foods span an almost continuous spectrum of quality. And though animal proteins are generally of higher quality than plant proteins, there is overlap: the quality of some cereal proteins, and of soya bean and cashew nut protein, is little inferior to that of meat or cheese protein.

Second, when we said that grain provides all the protein an adult needs, we had already made adjustments for protein quality. Thus wheat protein has a relative deficiency of lysine, and less than half the amount of protein consumed is utilized. But the concentration of protein in wheat is around 13 per cent; so despite this lack of quality, the utilizable amount remains above the required 5 per cent. We still do not need to worry too much about protein if we have a wheat-based agriculture.

Third, different plant proteins can complement each other. One of many favours that nature has conferred upon the human race is to make bean protein rich in lysine: hence if beans are eaten together with cereal, the deficiency of the latter is to some extent made good, and the quality of its protein increased. This is yet another reason for including beans in our rational agriculture. And as we will see in Chapter VII, the bean-cereal combination has played a major part in all the world's great cuisines.

Finally, meat tends to contain a relative surplus of essential amino acids. Meat eaten in small quantities with cereal, bean, or potato, tends again to increase their protein quality. Putting it another way – to cite the United Nations Protein Advisory Group – meat protein is utilized most efficiently when eaten in conjunction with plant protein; after all, if meat is eaten alone, then a proportion of all its essential amino acids is wasted.[43]

Hence we again see that the products of rational agriculture – small amounts of meat supplementing grain, potato, and bean – perfectly match human nutritional requirements, as laid down by the most modern and convincing nutritional theory, including our protein requirements. The neatness of the fit seems too good to be true: but as we will see in Chapter VI, this close fit is perfectly explicable on evolutionary grounds.

But one other nutritional idea, with which our rational agriculture is also in accord, deserves mention. This is the idea that health in general and body weight in particular may be greatly affected by the proportion of fibre in the diet.

The fibre hypothesis is undermined by doubtful pedigree. Coarsely termed 'roughage', fibre has been widely regarded primarily as a spur for recalcitrant bowels, bound by mythology to the cold shower and the *lederhosen*. Conventional nutritionists looked up from their test-tubes and said that since fibre was chemically inert, and present in food only in small amounts, and since none of their trials with rats and children demonstrated any clear advantage in eating it, it could safely be classified with royal jelly, honey, and dried sea-weed: a harmless enough indulgence that might do you good if you believed in it. Clinicians treating gut disease tended, if anything, to suggest that since fibre is largely cellulose and cellulose is indigestible, it was more likely to abrade the gut than sooth it, and should be avoided.

Renewed interest in fibre has developed through several distinct disciplines: epidemiology, physiology, biochemistry, microbiology and clinical medicine. The ideas are still very much in the melting pot; many scientists and doctors have contributed, and it is difficult to give proper credit to all involved. But most of the fibre enthusiasts emphasize their debt to Surgeon-Captain T. L. Cleave, one of the rare and valuable breed of clinician-scholars.[44]

Cleave noted that people in 'developed' societies suffer diseases that in 'primitive' or less affluent societies are rare or non-existent. Among these 'diseases of affluence' are several in which diet is impli-cated: these include coronary heart disease, diabetes, and a catalogue of gut diseases including diverticulitis and cancer of the colon. He suggested that one of the most consistent differences between the diets of societies that suffered 'diseases of affluence', and those that did not was the amount of fibre each contained. Fibre consists of the skeletal elements of plants: cellulose, hemicelluloses, pectins and so-called lignins. People are able to eat low-fibre diets only if they are well-nigh carnivorous, or if the fibre is removed from the plant material by milling or other kinds of refining. Among people who rely heavily on plants for food – which includes practically everybody except the Eskimo, Masai and a few others – a low-fibre diet has been possible only as a result of radical food processing in the past 150 years, to produce sugar and white flour. Cleave argued that human beings simply were not adapted, through evolution, to consume a low-fibre diet.

The idea has two aspects. First, it is now widely argued that fibre has positive effects on gut function, and that its simple absence may lead to disease. Second, Cleave pointed out that in nature it is almost impossible for human beings or animals to obtain carbohydrate in large amounts without simultaneously imbibing large amounts of fibre.

Honey and dates are two of the very few wild sources of concentrated sugar: neither play a large part in the diets of most human beings. Only by knocking off the bran of wheat, or squeezing the pulp from sugar cane or beet, is it possible to provide humans with large amounts of 'refined' carbohydrate. The human body simply is not equipped to cope with this entirely novel and highly influential item of food.

The significance of fibre *per se* is still controversial. But intriguing and probably significant facts have been established. We know that 'fibre' is highly heterogeneous, and that the stuff that old-style nutritionists termed 'roughage' is only a small part of it. Nutritionists conventionally measured the fibre in food by dissolving away the rest with acid and alkali, and seeing what was left. But this leaves only the cellulose intact. We now know that the hemicelluloses that are destroyed by this crude extraction process constitute the bulk of dietary fibre. Hence the 'crude fibre' (cellulose) content of wholemeal flour may be only 2 per cent; the 'dietary fibre' content – including the hemicelluloses – may be 12 per cent.[45]

The cellulose and hemicelluloses exert their influence through the full length of the gut – unlike most other dietary components which are extracted in the stomach and small intestine. Thus fibre has a particularly significant effect on the colon – the large bowel. And it is now clear that the colon is not the metabolically uninteresting sponge-like tube it has sometimes been taken to be: among other things, it controls the circulation and chemical composition of bile salts which pass from body to gut and back again; and these salts profoundly influence liver metabolism.[46] We also know that the important hemicelluloses are not chemically inert: they are broken down by intensive bacterial action. Their presence or absence can be shown to have an enormous effect on the chemical and bacterial activities within the colon. Some of the diseases of affluence are specifically colon diseases. No one is yet able to state categorically that lack of fibre causes them, but since fibre does so profoundly influence the general environment of the colon only a bigot (and bigots are by definition unscientific) would deny that it could be important.

Fibre also has more obvious effects. High-fibre diets, in general, tend to pass through the gut much more quickly than low-fibre diets: [47] total passage time on an African villager may be only one-third that of a westerner. The resultant changes in the chemistry of the colon may or may not be clinically significant; they certainly are worth taking seriously. Similarly, the light-weight bulk of fibre evidently makes it easier for the colon to shuttle its contents along – and bran is now

C*

widely used, particularly in Britain, in treating people with such colonic disorders as diverticular disease. The fact that bran eases the condition does not prove that lack of bran caused it. But the idea that there is a cause and effect relationship deserves to be looked at closely.

However, this is not meant to be a textbook on fibre: there are already several, and the next few years will see many more. Suffice it to say that fibre is not mere roughage, and that interest in it is absolutely not the prerogative of cranks.

The correlative idea – that the removal of fibre makes it possible to eat large amounts of refined carbohydrate, and that this may be harmful – has little support in the way of hard experimental data, but a great deal in the way of common sense, and of broad clinical and epidemiological observation. Cleave suggested that rapid ingestion of a high concentration of dietary sugar made possible by carbohydrate refinement could directly influence and upset the delicate blood-sugar control mechanisms, centred around the insulin-producing cells of the pancreas. Thus, he suggested, refined carbohydrate could play a part in causing diabetes – and certainly this disease is common in 'civilized' societies, and rare or non-existent among the less developed.

More straightforward is the idea emphasized by Drs Ken Heaton[48] and Hugh Trowell.[45] They have each pointed out that a human being, or any other animal, has very delicate mechanisms for controlling its appetite. Only domestic livestock and civilized man grow fat. But how does the body know when it has had enough? An immensely complex question, but one of the cues which says 'stop eating!' is the feeling of satiety that comes from sheer bulk. Bulk, as far as plant foods are concerned, is largely fibre. Take out the fibre, and you have removed a crucial component of appetite control.

The average Englishman eats an astonishing five ounces (140 g) of refined sugar every day – most of it merely as titillation for the taste buds. To eat the same amount of sugar in unrefined form he would have to eat, say, three pounds (1·4 kg) of apples. The American who takes a can of cola with his meal takes in 38 grams of sugar: commensurate with 7 ounces (200 g) of peeled banana, 12 ounces (340 g) of apples, or 14 ounces (400 g) of pears.

So if the average Englishman or American is to stay a reasonable weight, he has to cut down on some other food if he wants to go on eating refined suger. Since the sugar does not satisfy his hunger pangs, this cutting down takes on the heroic character of dieting. We have already seen, too, that if he keeps within a reasonable intake of calories, yet eats sugar, which unlike wheatflour has no accompanying protein, then he has to eat correspondingly greater amounts of high-protein food, such as meat, to keep his energy-protein balance right. (By a 'reasonable' intake of calories, I mean the amount that would keep you at your optimum weight. And by optimum weight, I mean the weight at which, for your height and age, the actuarial tables beloved of insurance companies suggest that you are least likely to die. Half the adult population in Britain, and probably a greater proportion of Americans, exceed this ideal weight by at least 10 per cent.)

But this thesis leads us to what conventional slimmers would consider a heresy. For the high-fibre diet that Heaton and Trowell advocate is a high-plant diet. And a high-plant diet is a high-carbohydrate diet. But almost every slimming buff there has ever been has told you to cut down on carbohydrates.*

Of course there is no paradox – so long as you distinguish between the unrefined carbohydrate of wholemeal bread, potatoes with their skins on, unpeeled fruit and the rest, and the refined carbohydrate of sugar and white flour. We have seen that these are very different entities.

And Hugh Trowell has pointed out that when he visited Uganda in the late 1920s – as a clinician, not a tourist – he never saw a fat African. The people were not short of food: indeed, as in many other societies, it was a mark of politeness to leave a full bowl at the end of the meal. Yet their diets were low in meat, high in grain and vegetable – and hence high in carbohydrate. But they were also high in fibre.

When Trowell revisited Uganda in 1970 he found thousands of fat Africans in Kampala. President Amin has the dimensions of a fairly typical urban African. Correspondingly, the diabetes clinics had sprung up like mushrooms in Kampala: diabetes is associated with obesity.

Closer to home, we find a report in the *New England Journal of Medicine*, 29 May 1975,[49] in which investigators from Harvard and elsewhere tested the effects of vegetarian diets on blood lipids. Their results on that score are not particularly striking: but their observation made in passing that people turning to a macrobiotic diet – high carbohydrate but also high fibre – finished up around 15 kg lighter than the controls, is highly intriguing. Few western slimmers, for all their

---

* I now learn – from *Medical World News*, 15 December 1975 – that the ITT Continental Baking Company of Rye, NY, is producing a 'high-fiber bread', with 'purified wood pulp' added to refined flour. With a little more technology, they might be able to imitate unrefined wheat flour almost exactly.

agonies, lose 15 kg – more than 30 lb. Yet these people weren't even trying to lose weight.

Professor John Yudkin has emphasized the refined carbohydrate story in *Pure, White and Deadly*. But whereas Cleave argued that human beings are ill-adapted specifically to refined carbohydrate, Yudkin at least suggests that human beings are ill-adapted to carbohydrate in general. He suggests that the men who first began arable farming around 15–10,000 years ago had hitherto been largely carnivorous, and that the ill-health now resulting from high intake of sugar is an aspect of the ill-health that might result from high intake of carbohydrate in general.[50]

I will argue in the next chapter that this view of evolution is highly romanticized and unnecessarily elaborate; and the idea that we are ill-adapted to carbohydrate in general hardly accords with the observation that people on natural high-carbohydrate diets can be extremely healthy. Granted, such people often live in the Third World, where infection, poverty, dirt and contamination take their toll and thus confuse the picture. But a well-fed African villager is a well-fed man, despite his massive carbohydrate intake.

Yudkin, of course, in *This Slimming Business*,[51] argues that the best way to get slim is to cut out carbohydrate altogether – although he allows fruit. The resulting high-meat, 'high-protein' diet evidently works. But in the modern world it is highly prodigal: paradoxically, the high-meat diet slimmer uses more agricultural resource than the conventional eater who gets his energy from bread and potatoes. The high-meat diet is also expensive. Nice to know it is unnecessary.

Our rational agriculture would keep extraneous processing to a minimum. There is no point in imposing technology between farm and consumer for the sake of it; and with our emphasis on local production, it becomes more difficult to effect the economies of scale on which processing largely depends. Both the emphasis on grains, potatoes, and beans, and the subsequent lack of processing, fit neatly with modern ideas on the benefits of fibre. Among other things, lack of processing and a curb on sucrose production could solve the west's obesity problem – sometimes said to be our greatest health problem – at a stroke.

But the argument begins to smack of wishful thinking. We devise an agriculture according to agronomic criteria, and then find it fits man's nutritional needs better than the present agriculture. Isn't this too good to be true?

Not at all. As we shall see in the next chapter, if you take a cool view of man's evolution, you would not expect anything else.

What Kind of Man
are You?

So far we have discussed nutrition disjointedly, seemingly with only a tenuous connection between the different parts. That the nutritional ideas fit in with our rational agriculture seems merely fortuitous. But if we integrate the ideas, we find the fit is perfectly logical.

Two questions. First, how can we tell whether a given diet is 'good' – whether modifications do or do not constitute improvement? Second, why do people eat the things they do – sometimes seeking food that may be harmful?

Both questions may be resolved into one: what kind of animal is the human being?

Let's take the first question first – how we know whether a diet is good or not. It is relatively easy to tell when people are acutely poisoned: the ancients knew a whole pharmacopoeia of toxins. It is much harder to discover deficiencies in diets: not till the eighteenth century was scurvy traced to a lack of something that occurs in citrus fruits (which we now know to be vitamin C, ascorbic acid) and obvious though the clinical signs of vitamin deficiency diseases may be, it was not till the twentieth century that they were understood; and the roles of vitamins E and K, and even of C, are still controversial. Even so, the shortfalls in diet caused by toxicity on the one hand, or vitamin deficiency on the other, are relatively easy to trace; both, at least in extreme form, produce obvious ill-health fairly quickly.

But human beings, in common with rats, pigs, and cockroaches, have an extraordinary capacity to survive on a great range of diets. And most people survive most of the time on whatever is to hand. Surely the science of nutrition should concern itself with more than mere survival? But unless a man becomes demonstrably ill, how can we judge whether his diet is poor, or could be improved?

The problem would be easy if we had a clear image of what human beings should be like; if we could say that a man should be six feet tall (1·83 m) at age 16, and 30 inches (76 cm) around the waist – just as agriculturalists prescribe the dimensions of the ideal pig, or dog breeders define the perfect poodle – then we would know what we were aspiring to. We might reasonably assert that the modern American diet, which does tend to produce men of around six feet,

is superior to that of Tudor England, in which even the well-fed aris-
tocracy rarely exceeded five foot six (1· 68 m).

But prescriptions of physical perfection in humans have the ring
of Nazi madness. And though twentieth-century paediatricians and
mothers have tended to emphasize the importance of high growth
rate in babies – the 'bouncing baby' after all, was an encouraging anti-
dote to the sickliness that was so common in the nineteenth century
– surely no one would assert that a man who manages to reach six
feet (1·83 m) is necessarily a better human being than he would have
been if he had remained four inches (10 cm) shorter. Most civilized
societies have rated other qualities – intelligence, humanity, longevity
– higher than mere size.

We gain some idea of whether people are thriving on their diet,
or merely surviving, if we look at them not individually, but en masse.
The actuarial tables of insurance companies tell us, for example, that
people around five feet eight (1·70 m) are least likely to die at a given
age if they weigh around eleven stone (70 kg). If they are significantly
heavier or lighter than this, their chances of dying increase commensurately. It seems perverse to argue that early death is a good thing,
so we might reasonably argue that a diet that tends to keep you at the
weight where your chances of survival are greatest, has merit.

Epidemiology – the study of disease patterns – tells us more. It tells
us, for example, that coronary heart disease is by far the biggest cause
of death in middle-aged western males – though people in many other
societies, such as African villagers, almost never die from it. Evidence
from many sources suggests that diet plays a part; again we can
reasonably assert that a diet that promotes such untimely death leaves
something to be desired.

But how do we make sense of this? Why should a rich diet, providing us with all the things humans are known to need, prove more
dangerous than an ostensibly poorer one? Almost to a man, biologists
and clinicians have sought the answer in man's evolution. After all,
they say, the diet of western man has changed radically since the beginning of the industrial revolution, since the growth of mass wealth
on the one hand and food refinement on the other, yet our bodies,
and particularly our guts, have not had time to alter correspondingly.
The first man-like creatures are known to have lived in Africa about
three million years ago. The first unmistakably human men – the first
who would not have attracted attention in a walk down Fifth Avenue
– have been dated from around 40,000 years ago. Evolution shaped
man's gut during that time. Primitive people who were not adapted

to the diet available during that time simply died out. In short, we should find out what primitive men ate, because we have inherited a gut that is adapted to their diet.

This line of reasoning is not faultless. After all, we live very different lives from primitive men. What suited them would not necessarily meet our needs. Again, primitive man really was 'concerned' only with survival: and survival only to reproductive age, which in our ancestors probably was usually less than 20 years. A diet that took them to 20 would not necessarily take us to 70. And we cannot assume that primitive men were themselves closely adapted to their diets: after all, dogs and cats can survive on garbage, but few would argue that this was their ideal food.

Yet the basic argument, that evolution shaped our metabolism to cope with the primitive diet, does make sense. It is worth asking what early men and pre-men ate. After all, the modern epidemiological evidence does intimate that our fundamental error is to stray from the primitive; the rough and ready diets of people who do not suffer coronary disease or diabetes are probably much more like the primitive diets than our own.

So let's bear the caveats in mind, but press on with our evolutionary investigations nonetheless. Unfortunately, most previous attempts to do this have gone disastrously wrong. The more or less undisputed facts are these. Man belongs to the order of mammals known as the primates: his modern relatives are apes, monkeys, and lemurs. The primates descended from tree-living insectivores – whose modern more direct descendants include tree shrews, shrews and moles. The ancient tree-living insectivores, like their modern survivors, presumably ate insects.

The primates are first and foremost forest creatures. But about three million years ago, as the forest began to shrink, a group in Africa began to spend more and more time on the ground. Some of these ground-apes were man-like; their descendants indeed evolved into men. They were successful, and spread all around the world; crucial modern barriers to travel, such as the Behring Straits and the English Channel, had not yet formed. About 15,000 to 10,000 years ago, independently in Central America, the Middle East, and the Far East, men became agricultural.

This historical sketch has been brightly coloured with a nutritional theory that runs roughly as follows. The primates from which men descended were allegedly vegetarian. The first men, on the other hand, were largely carnivorous; they could not have found enough vegetation for subsistence on the plains they had come to inhabit, and their early interest in weaponry suggests a killer streak. In addition, hunting, especially for a small ape-like creature not over-endowed with tooth and claw, requires cunning and organization. Meat eating requires tools to sever skin and sinew; and creatures not equipped with the ultra-powerful protein-digesting enzymes found in the guts of cats or dogs quickly learnt the benefits of fire, to break down and soften the flesh. Hunting encouraged manual dexterity, and, commensurately, cerebral development. When man became agricultural, during the neolithic revolution, his diet changed again: he became more emphatically vegetarian, relying heavily on seeds, particularly grains, as staple.

Professor Yudkin, author of *Pure, White and Deadly* and *This Slimming Business*, cited in the last chapter, favours this kind of interpretation. From it, he seeks to explain the apparent association between the 'diseases of affluence' and the high intake of refined carbohydrate. He suggests that man did not eat carbohydrate at all in large quantities until he became agricultural, by which time he was already adapted to a high-meat diet; hence he is ill-adapted to a high-carbohydrate diet.

Yudkin explains western man's apparent predeliction for meat in the same terms. We have inherited the guts and instincts of primitive men who for most of their evolution were largely carnivorous. In agricultural societies, meat is hard to come by – unless that society grows rich. And when societies do grow rich, meat eating increases: the primitive urges are unleashed – set free by opportunity. History does seem to be on his side: societies do seem to eat more meat as they grow wealthier, as has happened in the US and western Europe this century, and is happening in the USSR and Japan today.

Yudkin's view of man's dietary evolution is widely accepted. It neatly explains man's intellectual breakaway from the rest of the primates and his present meat-eating leanings. Yet I think the idea is largely bunkum. Some of the underlying assumptions are false – a bad start for any scientific hypothesis – and the reasoning is over-elaborate. Good scientific hypotheses, above all, are economical.

For a start, the idea that the primates from which man descended were vegetarians is not soundly based. Zoologists thought modern primates were vegetarians until recent decades – as, indeed, conspicuous representatives such as the orang-utan and gorilla apparently are. But monkeys, before the war, pined in zoos for lack of protein and they are now fed high-protein supplements – which true vegetarians should not need. And modern observation in the field (careful field observation of mammals is a recent phenomenon) show that some groups of chimpanzees,[52] and olive baboons,[53] do not simply eat meat, but actually hunt. In short, primates as a group are not vegetarian, but omnivorous – even though, as forest dwellers, they may have vegetarian leanings, and even though some types seem almost exclusively vegetarian.

But we can reasonably assume that the first pre-men to leave the forest did not suddenly switch to meat eating. They were already omnivorous; they already ate some meat. And we cannot assume that they relied solely on meat eating. After all, as hunters in Africa they would have competed with lion, leopard, and hunting dog: a formidable opposition. And they would have hunted creatures that were equipped to escape such predators. Monkeys, young animals, wounded large mammals would have been the most obvious prey. Scavenging would have provided no easy entry into carnivorousness, as the van Lawick-Goodalls point out in *Innocent Killers:* [54] the lions, leopards, and dogs also compete for carrion, together with the hyaena, with its formidable jaws. It seems beyond question that the first pre-men hunted, and that hunting subsequently played a large part in their lives: but common sense, and observation of modern primitive peoples such as the Kalahari bushmen and the Australian aborigine, suggests that they were first and foremost omnivorous, albeit placing greater emphasis on meat than their forest ancestors.

And did the switch to agriculture really produce a dramatic change in diet? The theory is that man first began to sow seeds when he noted, by chance, that the ones he dropped after he had gathered them, germinated. It hardly seems likely that he would ever have got around to dropping them, or taken much interest in their fate, if he was not already interested in food plants. Again we note that today's primitive hunter-gatherers, including the peoples of the Amazon basin, have a detailed knowledge of the local plant life.

And the first farmers – at least in the Middle East – do not seem to have been emphatically arable. Archaeological evidence of domestic and semi-domestic stock – sometimes including creatures such as the antelope which are only now coming back into favour – dates virtually from the beginning of agriculture. The Old Testament, after all, has as many references to shepherds as to corn; Cain's favoured brother, Abel, was a pastoralist.

In short, I suggest that omnivorous hunting-gathering man graduated untraumatically into omnivorous agricultural man; and that the first agricultures were no more than a mirror held up to the nature to which he was adapted.

Thus, the difference between the primitive diet, to which man might be adapted, and the modern western one, to which he apparently is not, is far more subtle than the gross difference between meat eating or not meat eating, or carbohydrate or non-carbohydrate. The differences lie in such cryptic parameters as the amount of fibre – as Cleave and his disciples suggest; or in the ratio of muscle fibre to saturated fat to polyunsaturated fat in the meat, as Crawford suggests. Such subtlety of difference, taken over a lifetime, is sufficient to explain the physical and pathological peculiarities of western modern man: his bulk, and his tenuous grasp on life after middle age.

And we can explain the growth of meat eating in rich societies – and all man's other dietary quirks as well – far more succinctly if we simply develop the idea that he is an omnivore, than we can by suggesting that his psyche is shot through with vestiges of earlier lifestyles.

The trouble is that biologists have tended to give omnivores short shrift. What are the characteristics of carnivores, they ask. And they list: weaponry; well-developed brains; jaws and teeth that move like scissors, to sever flesh; short guts exuding fierce acids and enzymes to dissolve it. Herbivores, on the other hand, have huge elongated guts, equipped with diverticular chambers to cope with cellulose; and high-crowned teeth and jaws to move them sideways like querns, to smash the fibre.

Omnivores, the conventional biology texts are apt to tell us, are mere middle-of-the-roaders. Man, a typical omnivore, can neither tear flesh nor crush herbage particularly well; but he can do both, after a fashion. His guts are neither particularly long, nor particularly short. Metabolically, he is a mediocrity.

Such nineteenth-century physiological musing loses sight of the fact that omnivorousness is the most sophisticated mode of all. Speaking anthropomorphically (in the interests of brevity), a carnivore knows what he has to do: if it moves, chase it. A herbivore sticks his head down, and becomes a grazer, or up, and becomes a browser. The herbivore may be highly selective: the sheep nibbling the grass tips, the horse ripping to the roots: but his selectivity is determined largely by the anatomy of his jaws, and he cannot do much about that.

To the omnivore, on the other hand, the whole environment is potentially edible. But equally, because it is full of poisonous roots and berries and leaves and insects, it is all potentially dangerous. Far more than the specialist feeders, the omnivore must explore his environment; but he must also be highly discriminatory, for he is far more likely, during his experimental feeding, to poison himself.

In practice, omnivores are experimental – but they are also conservative. In general, they tend to select a short catalogue of items from the many thousands that their environment often presents them with – and then stick to it. We see this experimental tendancy tempered by conservatism in omnivores far lowlier than man. Even though rats can adapt to almost any diet – one reason for their survival in sewers, and their usefulness as laboratory fodder – they are extraordinarily difficult to poison in the wild. Introduce succulent bait into their environment, and they ignore it. Only after several days will the rat come to accept that what is ostensibly esculent can be safely consumed. At a higher level, we find that different tribes of baboons or apes, even though living in similar environments, select different diets. Some groups accept one lot of items as good, safe, tested nutrients; and others, with a different range of experience, select others.

The human shows the same tendencies as other omnivores. The evolutionary need to be discriminatory leads him to seek clear, distinct flavours that he can easily recognize again, and which he knows are not associated with poison. In the wild, sweet things fulfil this function: honey and fruit provide energy, and sweet fruit at least tends to be edible. Bitter things often fill the opposite function: they are often poisonous.

In practice today we find people latching on to the clear recognizable flavours of onion, garlic, sugar, tea, coffee, chocolate and bananas; and in the west, meat. For a primitive man living in a primitive world, with no tea, coffee or chocolate, or pure sugar, such primitive discrimination helps to keep him reasonably on the rails, nutritionally. In a modern society, the tendency to latch on to such flavours can lead him astray. Hence the Baganda tribe of Uganda are hooked on bananas, and regularly eat six or more pounds a day – to their nutritional detriment.

The food industry knows full well that the omnivore seeks palatal stridency. *The Wall Street Journal* of April 1974 told how a manufacturer had failed to sell a tomato sauce that tasted of tomatoes. As *The Times* subsequently commented,[55] 'it lacked the over-cooked, scorched flavour of the most popular sauces, which is what makes them tasty and popular.' The scorched tang of the artificial flavouring relates to the tomato as the saloon piano to the clavicord; and succeeds for the same reason, that you are caught up by its vampish insistence.

The evolutionary need to be conservative causes omnivores to stick to what they know. On the negative side, this causes primitive peoples to eat only a small selection – rarely more than 10 per cent – of the theoretically edible components of their environment. Things not included on their list of accepted foods are simply non-food. Thus the Jews and Moslems eschew pork, and the Hindu, beef. Thus, too, attempts to introduce more productive strains of rice or whatever into Third World societies have often failed because the people do not accept innovation. Thus, too, the French have often regarded maize – a staple in parts of South America – merely as cattle food; but they relish horsemeat, which the English reserve for dogs and Belgians.

On the positive side, people generally adapt to the gastronomic norms of their society. You might not like tripe and onions: whole generations of Lancastrians have learned to love them. I found the smoked lamb and raw fish of Iceland a little powerful; the Icelanders clearly do not. The food industry understands our innate conservatism, too. As Charles Grimm, director of Flavour Creation, of International Flavors and Fragrances Inc, New York, told *The Times*: 'people like what they are familiar with. Younger people today don't know what percolated coffee tastes like. They're all used to soluble coffee. And they don't know what fresh pineapple juice tastes like. They're used to canned pineapple juice where the flavour is affected by the can.' Artificial flavouring was, he said, 'a very expanding industry'.

In general, I suggest that the gastronomic predilections and aversions of a child, at weaning, are more or less a *tabula rasa*. He may grow up with an exaggerated love of peanut butter, or an aversion to carrots, but in general he will adapt quickly to what is around. That is the fundamental characteristic of omnivores – that they adapt to what is around. Taboos and addictions, both, are merely extreme manifestations of the adaptive process led astray by circumstance.

What about increased meat eating in rich societies? We have already observed, in Chapter III, that agriculture has to produce more meat as society grows richer in order both to cope with its own overproductiveness, and to add value to its produce commensurate with the wealth of the rest of society. A whole generation of westerners have adapted to this surfeit, just as other generations adapted to its lack.

Of course people like meat. It belongs in the category of distinct dietary entities, which omnivores are genetically programmed to seek. Also – because meat eating has generally been the prerogative of the rich – meat has kudos. The modern middle class likes to regale its guests with meat – not least as a symbol of generosity. And meat is 'promoted': though things have changed since Britain joined the EEC, I used to pass, on my way up the escalator, a series of exhortations to eat Polish ham, Danish bacon, Irish beef, and New Zealand lamb. Now the small ads are all for panti-hose and hair transplants – but the television has recently (October 1975) urged us to 'buy a bigger piece' – of British beef. Steak houses have sprung up partly because steak does not require expensive cooks – it merely needs a few heaters-up, who are often immigrants paid a derisory wage. In short, the idea that the meat cult has grown up spontaneously in the west, in response to 'public demand' – a demand, furthermore, that is supposed to be engraved by evolution on our psyche – is ludicrous. Meat has been 'sold', at least in Britain in my lifetime, as assiduously as any other commercial product and already enjoyed an exaggerated status that resulted from over-reaction to the poverty and inequity of an earlier age. As good omnivores, we have adapted.

What evidence is there, outside the western growth economy and those influenced by it – including those Third World countries trying to copy us – of an overweening love of flesh? Children, in my experience, do not take more readily to meat than to other things. They certainly do not cry out for lean: they like (as I liked as a child) the crispy bits, the slivers of burnt tendon next to the knuckle. Peking mandarin gourmets, who could have had whatever they liked, allegedly ate only the skin of the duck, and gave the flesh to the servants. No innate love for the flesh here. Brillat Savarin, who carried his obsession for food through the French Revolution (athletically changing sides on the way) writes of saddle of mutton, and hare, and odd cuts of this and patés of that:[56] no emphatic exhortation of the beefsteak here, either.

History does not show that the west's modern carnivorousness is rooted in anything deeper than commercial expediency, linked to mankind's innate obligingness to adapt. Exactly the same line of argument explains our predilection for the other manifestations of value-adding – tea, coffee, tobacco, sugar, and the rest. Those who seek to explain our increased meat eating as a vestige of early carnivorousness must invoke a totally different explanation of our parallel increase in sugar or tobacco consumption – unless we are to suppose that early men were heavy smokers too. Scientific hypotheses that must make a separate case for each apparently related phenomenon are innately flawed.

The spectacle of biologists rushing to justify prevailing commercial circumstances in evolutionary terms is not new: in the last century, scientists as distinguished as Thomas Huxley explained the suppression of Africans and Asians in terms of their racial inferiority. But it is not an edifying spectacle. Bad anthropological theory helped to bolster the prejudice that has impeded world political progress; and bad nutritional theory, confusing market growth with innate psychological need, now helps to impede progress in agriculture.

In short, we are well adapted to the products of rational agriculture; to unrefined carbohydrate, small garnishings of meat, and the rest. But won't we die of boredom? Can this nutritious diet be exciting?

Read on.

The Great Cuisines
are Waiting

Nutritionists are wont to paint a picture of the healthy life in which masochism stands well to the fore. School marms exhort us to eat up our overdone spinach, while vegans regale us with an endless round of muesli and nutburgers. Gastronomes too often present food as pure sensation, with little thought for the whole man and none for the world in which he lives. Thus has the cause of good nutrition been perverted by the faddist and the bossy dietician, and gastronomy shamefully corrupted by the food snob.

But the products of our rational agriculture are not the foundations of a mere food fad. We have grains, beans, and potatoes for basic nourishment; plenty of fresh vegetables and fruit, and modest but appreciable amounts of lean meat, from many species and all parts of the animal, to fill in the nutritional cracks and add the essential element of pleasure. We have home-grown herbs – for many of which the harshest climates are adequate, and for others of which micro-climates, found almost everywhere, will suffice. We have small quantities of imported spice and fruit – those high value, small volume crops that tropical countries can produce for monetary gain without perverting the structure of their own rational agriculture.

We have, indeed, the basis for all the world's great peasant cuisines: not surprising, since those cuisines have been evolving for at least 15,000 years to exploit the products of modest agriculture to the best advantage. And from peasant cuisines have grown the best of grande cuisine, as the great cooks – Fanny Craddock, Elizabeth David, Jane Grigson, Robert Carrier, Margaret Costa, Kenneth Lo – constantly emphasize: and we can say goodbye to much of what now passes as grande cuisine, overladen with double cream, without a tear. We have nothing to fear. We have only to re-learn how to cook.

In the great cuisines grain is often used as grain – as in the rice of South East Asia, the pearled barley in British stews, or as oatmeal in Scotland. Time and again we see the more or less unprocessed grain – used after no more than a cursory milling – garnished with small amounts of meat: precisely the meat-plant protein balance now recommended to make best use of the former and guarantee the nutritional quality of the latter. Hence the pulaos and biryanis of

India; the dolmades – finely comminuted meat with spice and rice in vine leaves – of Greece; and its almost exact equivalent in Scotland, the haggis, where liver, lung, and what you will are married with oatmeal. Haggis is both a gastronomic and nutritional triumph – and loses nothing, except in ethnic purity, in being matched with chips (French fries) in Glasgow. In general the cuisine of Scotland, developed by an ingenious people through hundreds of years of extreme austerity, deserves close study.

Of the major grains – rice, wheat, and maize – only wheat seems to me to lack something when cooked in its pristine state. It tastes well, though powerful, but takes a long time to cook and tends to remain too chewy (for my taste). I can find little evidence that wheat, as wheat, has extensively featured in peasant cuisine. But agriculturalists – who in Britain are now encouraged by the government to make their research more relevant to people's needs – might do worse than develop strains that can be cooked as easily as rice.

However, I have found that if half the wheat grains are first smashed in the spice grinder, mixed with the rest of the whole 'berries', and then broiled in a dry skillet till it pops to bring out the nuttiness; then lightly fried and then boiled in about three-and-a-half times the volume of water for an hour or so, the result is a good complement to, for example, mackerel. Macrobiotic cooks make much of wheat: their recipes, involving spices and vegetables, are worth a look. The issue is not vital – but it is irritating that the world's great cuisines have apparently made so little of what could be an interesting resource.

Grain in a slightly more comminuted form, or deliberately bred for glutinousness, becomes the basis of the Chinese 'rice gruels', or congees, tricked out with liver, shellfish, cabbage, or what you will; of the Chinese thick sweet-corn soups; and of Scottish porridge, made with oats. Again it would be nice if wheat could be used in this way, and the range of oats extended. The congee is a delightful form, and rational agriculturalists should not need recourse to imported rice.

Grind grain a little more – into flour – and we move into a whole new area. The list of cakes, pastries, noodles and bread is far too extensive to treat in detail. But let us note that the Englishman's almost exclusive concentration on wheat flour is a sad restriction. It is less notable in the US, where corn and rye-bread flourish; or in Scotland where the oatcake in its many variants lives on.

Note too how the products of the baker's shop have been sadly down-graded by the protein myth. The conventional view of the meat pie, for example, is that the pastry acted merely as 'stodge', to keep the gravy in. The modern view is that meat and pastry protein complement each other, while the starch in the pastry provides the energy that 'spares' the protein. In a sweet biscuit, the sugar pushes the energy-protein ratio too far in the energy direction; and in the Dundee cake, rich in eggs, the balance is restored. In the batter of Yorkshire pudding, or of pancakes, or used to coat vegetables or meat in deep-fries, the balance is restored with interest. Batters deserve more attention: toad-in-the-hole, where sausages lurk in a modified Yorkshire pudding, is potentially as versatile as the pizza.

Bread, with the protein myth killed, is restored to its rightful position as the staff of life. Modern millers, who insist on removing both the bran and the wheat germ to produce the ultra-white 70 per cent sponge rubber loaf that we are allegedly so fond of, succeed both in purging the fibre – which if left would ensure that bread need not be fattening – and in reducing the protein, mineral and vitamin content. They do this primarily for commercial reasons which we will examine in a later chapter. In sawing through life's staff they have a lot to answer for.

In bread – including the chapatis, nans, parathas and the rest, of India; the pitta of Greece; the tortilla of Mexico and so on – we see one of those reiterations of themes that makes the study of world cooking so fascinating. A similarly reiterated theme is the dumpling – the steamed stuffed dumplings of the wheat belt of China, also flourish in various forms in eastern Europe, and in the great meat or leek puddings of the north of England, where the basic flour and water is given body by the hard fat of suet. And suet pastry – baked now, rather than steamed – is used in one of the most economical and succulent dishes of all Europe, the potato pie of Lancashire. The basic ingredients of beef, perhaps kidney, and potato, onion, with loads of pepper and salt, cooked in a flower-pot shaped 'turtle' pot and left to simmer for hours in the slow oven by the perpetual coal fires of the mining towns, combine in the way that is characteristic of all classic dishes: the whole far exceeds, in flavour, the sum of its parts. Nutritionally the dish is unimpeachable. And it was born of austerity.

I doubt whether wholemeal flour, for all its nutritional and other technical advantages, should wholly replace white flour. It would be a shame to sacrifice the steamy lightness of a Chinese dumpling, for example. But whether the modern '70 per cent' flour is ever justified is a moot point: the British wartime 80–85 per cent flour, creamier in colour and with some of the bran and germ left in, seems as versatile. But a kitchen without wholemeal flour needs radical overhaul; wholemeal pastry, especially when heavily seasoned, gives an exciting edge to many a pie or pastie, while wholemeal apple crumble (the skins left on the apples and the pips left in) far outstrips the usual form. Persist with wholemeal flour; use it, and wholemeal bread if you can get it, wherever possible. It will reward you gastronomically, as well as nutritionally.

Pulses, and in particular beans, which should play such an important part in our rational agriculture and diet, are under-used and often notoriously abused by over-refined and under-informed western cooks. Nobody with a feel for cooking let alone an iota of nutritional knowledge, could regard the food industry's present obsession with soya steak and other ersatz bean products with anything other than bewildered disdain. How the US, which gave us the Boston baked bean – sweetened with molasses and tomato, buffered by onion and garlic, and edged with mustard and pepper – can take ersatz seriously is almost beyond understanding. I will return to this theme later. Let us first look at what real food experts can do with beans.

According to Jane Grigson,[57] 'every civilization has its special beans. Europe's classical bean, back to the Greeks, was the broad bean. The bean of the Incas, and the Mexicans, was the kidney-bean, which Peruvian Indians were eating several thousand years ago.' The Americans can also make use of the soya, whose possibilities are already demonstrated by China and perhaps even more by Japan (though the soya steak manufacturers like to pretend the pristine bean is unpalatable), and most countries have peas and lentils.

Good cooking, traditionally, reflects the seasons: the modern obsession for food out of season, or out of place, is little more than snobbery, which is another word for philistinism. The executive who flits from four-star hotel to four-star hotel, demanding Scotch steak, French château wine, Pacific prawns and out of season strawberries is not a gastronome, but a kind of junkie, the up-market equivalent of the Coca-cola-peanut butter addict. His basic lack of appreciation is reflected in his dumb acceptance of over-bred, over-frozen and over-boiled vegetables. But we can follow the seasons through beans, as witness a small quote from Jane Grigson: 'Beans of all kinds are a favourite accompaniment to lamb in France. In early summer there will be a dish of the beautiful stringless haricots verts. They will be followed by shelled green flageolet beans, first fresh, then half dried as summer passes. In winter the lamb will be served on a bed of white haricot beans. Sometimes they will be cooked together . . .', and she offers a recipe with garlic, onion, and carrot. There is, of course, room for lamb in rational agriculture. Especially when 'extended' – to borrow the food technologists' jargon – by beans.

Beans, like grains, may be more and more finely reduced, until you wind up with purées – a purée of lentils is a fine foil for sausages – or, more arcanely, with bessan, the bean flour of India. Usually they should not, as many food writers irritatingly insist, be soaked overnight; left so long they may begin to ferment, which spoils the flavour. Two hours is generally enough, and this may be shortened if they are brought to the boil and then left in the cooling water.

We have seen that beans, rich in lysine, complement cereal, which tends to be short of it. Obligingly, the cereal-plus-bean theme features in all the great cuisines. In China and Japan delicate beans complement rice. Dhalls, of infinite variety, are matched with chapatis in India, where bessan flour may also complement cereal flour in breads. The Mexicans wrap beans in tortillas (small boys thrived on this in John Steinbeck's *Tortilla Flat*, much to the nutritionists' astonishment) while bread and beans feature in a hundred combinations all around the Mediterranean. Beans and barley rub shoulders in many a stew in Britain, which is also the traditional home of beans on toast. I have matched haricot beans with pigeon and carrot and plenty of onion and garlic in a pie; the crust well-seasoned wholemeal. This, small fragments of wild meat extended two ways by cereal and bean is agronomic and nutritional perfection. My guests kept coming back for more.

In the trial of traditional nutritionists, no charge is more serious than their erstwhile abuse of the potato. It should be regarded as a staple, and as a source of protein, to rank with cereal. The idea that potatoes are fattening hardly accords with the observation that protein and calorie ratio approximates to human needs: obviously you will get fat if you eat too much. Perhaps the mistake has been to take off the fibrous skin. I commend Robert Carrier's advice[58] – 'whenever possible, cook potatoes in their jackets' – and suggest that the skins can be left on more often than you think. Try cooking unpeeled but coarsely chopped potatoes in a casserole with half an inch of water in the oven while the joint cooks. Add carrot, or onion, or parsnip, or turnip, or even whole tomatoes and a half cabbage on top for good measure – and then mix the resultant vegetable juice with the meat juice for gravy, with a bit of seasoning. An ancient technique of gravy-making;[59] in vivid contrast to the usual boiling and eleventh-hour resuscitation with proprietary gravy mix.

The potato's versatility is second only to that of cereals and no nation has employed it more ingeniously than the Swiss. One of Switzerland's many potato dishes – which I select because I think it is improved by including the skins, though most recipes recommend peeling – is rösti. One method is to boil the potatoes, let them cool, then slice them very thinly and fry in the fat of your choice, at first tossing them to get the crispy bits into the middle, and then pressing together so that the slices meld into a flat cake. Purists may question the technique, but it works, and cheese, herbs, or what you will, provide endless variations.

Swiss cuisine seems underrated, but anyone trying to get the best out of a temperate agriculture should look at it closely.[60] The Swiss use of soft fruits to make hard liquor should be studied in Britain and the US where the excursion into spirits perversely seems to begin and end with grain, potatoes, and juniper berries.

What of vegetables other than the pulses? I shall return to them in a later chapter. Suffice it to say that the variety that can be produced seasonally and locally is usually far greater than you imagine. Even in Britain, in April and May, the traditional months of the 'hungry gap', there are broccoli, several varieties of cabbage, spinach, late sprouts, and a wide variety of roots still left in store.

In short, our rational agriculture does not require asceticism. In demanding intelligent extension of what can be produced in the home country, and of what is in season, it merely accords with the fundamental principles of good cooking. In English middle-class homes I have been expensively treated to aubergine and pepper. All very well, but would a Provençale peasant, on whose cuisine the dishes are based, use anything that did not grow in his own fields? Britain does not have the world's most favoured climate; but even in that unpromising island, we could emulate most of the great cuisines of the world, not by borrowing foreign ingredients (except for the odd spice and orange) but by borrowing only the techniques. Great cooking is eclectic in ideas. In raw materials it is chauvinistic.

You may still have doubts, I suspect; on the grounds that traditional grain-and-potato cuisines are fattening. The nutritional answer – that high-carbohydrate foods with the fibre in are a world apart from refined carbohydrate – has been covered. I should add that the task of feeding anyone who resolutely declines to take exercise, is chauffeur driven and electrically elevated from bed to office chair, without making him fat, is physiologically impossible unless he curbs his appetite by iron will.

But one of the main reasons why modern food seems so fattening is that it is designed to be eaten to excess. Specifically, we find the food industry pushing food with little bulk and high-energy content, and known to be addictive, such as sweets, Coca-cola, sugary pop-corn, and ice cream. More generally, we have evolved the idea that part of civilized living is to eat like a mediaeval baron every day. The modern evening meal among the middle class in Britain, and increasingly among the working class, is 'dinner' – a hot meal built around meat. The modern 'convenience food' industry is largely based on attempts to provide this unlikely meal without effort.

Yet 'dinner' is only one form among many possible. Among many sections of the British working class, the traditional evening meal is high tea. This, like all good cuisine, is infinitely variable, yet fundamentally simple. With odd bits of meat or fish or egg matched with bread and cake it is well balanced nutritionally, and has the gastronomic virtues of reflecting location and season: a Devonshire tea is different, in detail, from a Yorkshire one.

And the high tea is 'convenient'. It was traditionally produced without too much time and trouble by women who often spent their days in factory or field. But the cooking of cakes and the like could be done on one day, for the whole week; and of pies and pastries, two or three times a week; or such things could be bought ready made, from the bakery. The great 'dinner', that westerners now like to eat every day, was reserved for one or two days a week, and for feast days.

The Victorian English upper middle class invented evening dinner. It passed the long evenings and there were plenty of servants to prepare and clear up. It was good gastronomy then, because it exactly suited the people's leisured life style. It is not appropriate to the life style of people who work all day; and the pastiches of the food industry, the not-so-instant instant mash and the pre-sliced beef, do not conceal its inappropriateness. A good tea is in a superior league to a bad dinner.

But the point here is that the Victorian dinner, with courses served à la Russe, was specifically designed to increase consumption. The dramatic switches from savoury to sweet and back again, were a device to overcome the feelings of satiety that comes from sameness as much as from volume. You do not need asceticism to avoid overweight, unless you are physiologically aberrant; but you do need to avoid gluttony, and gluttony is built into the Victorian dinner. Simplicity is the key to good eating, except on feast days.

Indeed, I suggest that the key to all crash slimming diets is ultra-simplicity: monotony. And this applies as much to the sophisticated diets based on beefsteak, as to the old-fashioned thin toast and black coffee. In some of the modern diets you are invited to eat as much as you like: provided it is only another grapefruit, or another sliver of cheese.

As a postscrpit, it would be good to see the restaurant more widely regarded as a place where good cooks nurtured the cuisines of their region, and where families went regularly to enjoy food and company. The most interesting restaurants in Holland, France, and Switzerland are of this kind. They are rare in the US and Britain. Too often in London the 'restaurant' is either an anonymous eating hall, for stoking up, or an expensive theatre of seduction where pretentious eclecticism fails to conceal the poverty of technique. Except for a few Chinese, Italian, and Greek restaurants, I know few where people would dream of taking their children. Sadly, on his rare days out, junior is marshalled into the hamburger joint.

Anyway, if we could only begin to see that cooking and eating are human-sized activities, necessary but also among our most pleasurable cultural indulgences; that it should not be regarded simply as a launching-pad for high technology and big business; then we need have no problems. We need not look to the high-flown nutritionists or faddists, and still less to the food industry, for guidance in an austere world. To misquote Winston Churchill, we merely need to put our faith in the people, for most of whom, through most of history, austerity has been a constant fact of life.

What of the food industry? Is it a help, or a hindrance? That I shall examine in the next two chapters.

viii

The Industrial Obstacle

The task is to grow the best food the land will produce, and cook it according to proven techniques. Conceptually straightforward. So where's the problem?

One problem, as we have seen, is that to farm according to the principles of good husbandry is no longer 'economic'; and to suggest we should do so is allegedly 'unrealistic'. Similarly, merely to cook the earth's produce makes no contribution to the economy – except, perhaps, in those periods of retrenchment (as in Britain, 1975) when politicians warn us that by subscribing to the growth economy we have overshot the mark, and must tighten our belts. We are assured, however, that the need to do rational things well is merely temporary: the next commercial genie (in Britain, 1975, it is North Sea oil) will put the Gadarene bandwagon back on its wheels.

Bestriding the modern food scene is the processing industry; whose most extreme manifestation is in 'convenience' food. Thirty-five per cent of the food now eaten in Britain is 'convenienced'; by the 1980s, we are joyfully informed, it will be 80 per cent, bringing Britain in line with the present-day US. This is 'an exciting growth area'.

The food processor is not merely a middle man. More and more food – the burgeoning soya acres of the US, the arable-style pea and blackcurrant fields of East Anglia – is grown specifically for his needs. Thus did Ernest Woodroofe, former chairman of the giant Unilever, parent of Birds Eye, explain the attraction of his job: 'The power to change things, the power not to have to accept things as they are . . . For instance, the agriculture of East Anglia has been altered by the operations of Birds Eye.' And a CIS report on Unilever added: 'In the UK alone Birds Eye now has over 1,000 farmers with exclusive contracts to sell it vegetables. Unilever supplies the seeds and technology, overseeing the whole operation, and helps arrange finance for the capital investments . . . To make profits under contract the farmer has to keep up with the technology, and so Unilever can industrialize farming by proxy.' We may add to that the research done by government as well as commercial agriculturalists, to breed the crops the industry needs.

And, of course, partly by conscious 'vertical integration', and partly through more subtle processes that I shall examine in later chapters, the processors increasingly control the activities of the 'retail outlets', and hence determine what is available to buy.

The processors have their critics, of course. 'Consumerism' is another growth area. The industries use of additives – about 3,000 different kinds in British food, and 3,890 in 1973 in the US[61] – is a prime target. Additives are important, and worth brief discussion, but they are no more than a symptom of a far more pernicious disease. The 'consumerists' are fighting the wrong battle. If I were an industrialist I would happily make concessions, most of which taken individually, would make little commercial difference, just to improve my image of responsible behaviour; an image that causes government and academics alike to shy from the attack that should be launched.

With regard to additives, the industry argues that they protect food – as when nitrites are used to prevent bacterial contamination of cooked meats; that some of the additives are nutrients – as when vitamin C is put in some brands of processed potato, or B vitamins in bread; that others stop things going stale, and that even those without such worthy intention, the colours and flavourings, reduce waste by enhancing palatability (and appearance is a large part of palatability, as good cooks recognize) and hence the likelihood of consumption.

Industrialists admit that they cannot provide absolute proof of the absolute safety of all additives, but point out, reasonably, that many 'natural' and accepted foods contain toxins – such as the oxalic acid in rhubarb – while other necessary foods, including table salt, are toxic if taken to excess (so is oxygen, incidentally). They add that traditional cooks have been using additives – including the maligned monosodium glutamate, the ve-tsin of Chinese cooking – since antiquity, so they are doing nothing new in principle: merely extending tradition with modern science. Objection is luddite and muddle-headed.

Finally, the industrialists point out, not without justification, that they now produce a large proportion of westerners' food – not simply the convenience foods, but also highly industrialized bread. Without additives, especially those that prolong shelf-life, the industry could not operate. Therefore, they imply, without additives, modern urban man would be deprived of a large proportion of his food supply. A few rich elites – like the health food buffs – may obtain additive-free food (though much of that is highly processed); but such food must remain the prerogative of the few. Hence objection to the additives that are the mainstay of the modern processor is both elitist and effete.

We may reply that the nutrients added to processed food are often – as with bread and 'instant' mashed potatoes – merely those removed by processing. Often, too, those put back by no means correspond to those removed. Hence the modern 70 per cent white loaf is deprived of some protein, and all the bran; the vitamin E, most of the B vitamin complex, including B_1, nicotinic acid, riboflavin, pantothenic acid, pyridoxine, and biotin; and much of the mineral salt – calcium, potassium, phosphorus, iron, copper, magnesium and manganese – that are present in whole flour. The industry puts back only powdered chalk (calcium), iron, nicotinic acid, and vitamin B_1. And those added – such as the B vitamin sometimes included in breakfast cereals – are not usually, or at least only by chance, those liable to be lacking in the consumer's diet; the choice of nutrients included is determined mainly by price.

In short, the nutrients are added usually only by way of compensation, or are merely gratuitous.

For the rest, we find that about 1,500 of the 3,000 used in Britain are purely cosmetic. The argument that these are not known to be dangerous – at the slightest hint of danger they are withdrawn – raises the question of how safety is tested. We saw in Chapter V that it took hundreds of years to show a clear relationship between the conspicuous disease of scurvy and the gross dietary defect – lack of vitamin C – that causes it; and indeed, that the relationship even between protein-lack and ill-health is not yet clear. With individual additives we are talking about micro-quantities, not given singly but in association with many others, which we will concede do not generally cause gross disease, but may have an effect over a lifetime. We would not expect to reveal a simple cause-and-effect relationship. And, as Dr James Thomson of the University of Surrey has pointed out, even with thalidomide, which in retrospect could be seen to have gross effects, and which, as a 'drug', was far more traceable than an additive, it took years to trace the cause and initiate action.[61]

It is, of course, logically impossible to demonstrate safety; toxicologists can demonstrate that a given material is not measurably toxic within the contexts of their experiments. Here we may observe – again quoting Thomson – that about 60 per cent of the additives now in use in Britain have been tested only for acute toxicity – not for long-term genetic or teratogenic effects that are more important to the human race. And when long-term tests are done – as is the case with all new

D

additives – they are done with laboratory animals; and thalidomide, which had no discernible effects on most of the animals it was tested on, shows how dangerous is the extrapolation from species to species.

The argument that 'natural' foods contain toxins is true, but raises the question of quantity. Each individual additive may be consumed only in trace amounts, but collectively we find that the average Briton consumes an estimated three pounds (1·4 kg) of additive a year – equivalent to 12 aspirin-sized tablets a day – and in the US the figure is nine pounds (4·1 kg): 36 'aspirins' per day. Even a certified rhubarb addict would be hard-pressed to match this.

As for the anti-staling agents and the rest that are so necessary to bring us food seemingly fresh, we may point out – as with the 'added' nutrients – that they are necessary only because the industrialist chooses to produce food in the centralized factory, distributing via the supermarket, where long shelf-life is essential. To take only one example, when people bought bread every day, fresh-baked, additives were not necessary. In any case, wholemeal stays palatable for days.

In truth, as I said, I do not believe the additive issue is of prime importance. The danger of being poisoned by an additive, albeit cryptically and long-term, seems to rank low in the catalogue of life's hazards. I present it partly to show how easily 'consumerist' arguments may be countered – and partly to show the extent to which the counter-arguments depend on half-truth.

The fundamental point is that almost all 'processing' – beyond that of traditional storage methods and the simple kitchen arts – is unnecessary in a rational food system, and that the industry's machinations are not to our benefit, but are merely devices that make it possible to impose industrial techniques on food production.

We must broaden the discussion. First let's ask, what does the food industry aspire to do? Second, does the food industry meet its own aspirations? Third, are the food industry's aspirations relevant to the creation of a rational food system? Fourth, if they are not, do they matter? Are they simply a side-issue, or do they impede progress towards a rational food system? Fifth, why does industry do the things it does? And, finally, how, if it does not always behave in society's interests, do the food processors succeed?

I shall answer these points in the next three chapters. To anticipate, I think it can be shown that the food industry's aspirations are largely trivial; that it does not succeed even in fulfilling them; that in their pursuit progress is impeded – that the industry is, indeed, the greatest single obstacle to rational food production; that it follows its extraordinary anti-social path not through perversity, but because it has mis-diagnosed the problems, and because it is impelled, inexorably, by commercial expediency; and that it succeeds only by the broadest based and most expensive system of advocacy ever conceived, a system that now embraces not only industry itself, but many of the theoretically alternative sources of information, including much of what in other spheres is recognizable as the independent academic world.

The Big Freeze, Ersatz
and Other Diversions

All food should be well cared for after harvest. Rats and mould and a host of insects in granaries, wind and flies among the dried fish catch in African open markets, fungus in stored fruit and roots, collectively dissipate up to 40 per cent of the harvest in some Third World countries; and the west is far from being immune. The solution is often technically simple, if expensive; a concrete parapet can exclude rats, or a wind-break save some of the dried fish. Sometimes – why not? – high science is appropriate: well-aimed chemistry can repel insects, the deep freeze will preserve oceanic fish, which have high nutritional and economic value (whatever the economic system), spoil quickly, and of necessity are caught spasmodically, in big lots.

Storage and food protection are aspects of 'processing'; even grain must be dried to the right degree – in the field if possible but by machine if not – and kept in a properly controlled atmosphere, if it is to remain wholesome for more than a few months. This chapter's condemnation of the modern food industry is not a blanket rejection of all processing, or of all high technology; that would be nonsensical. It is an objection to processing techniques inappropriately applied: to fulfil unnecessary or pernicious ideals, or to do necessary things by circuitous and profligate methods, primarily for no better reason than to graft the rationale of big business onto food production.

The food industry – Unilever, Ranks Hovis McDougall, Armour Foods, and, now, the giant oil companies – emphasize four major growth areas, all of which are the products of high technology, and are rooted only loosely in technique and rationale, in the methods of the past. The industry's oft-mooted point – that its techniques merely extend tradition – is at best only half true, as we shall see.

The favoured areas are 'convenience' foods; frozen foods; ersatz meat made from beans; and protein made from 'unconventional' sources, such as yeast protein produced on oil, or protein-rich fungi raised on plantation or industrial waste. Some of these techniques might find a limited role in a rational food system – though they should never be more than the gilt on the gingerbread. But collectively these innovations are a pernicious diversion, turning agricultural and scientific effort to irrelevant and increasingly trivial ends, and tending to obliterate the techniques and resources that could support a well-fed population in a stable world.

The claims made for convenience and deep-freeze products – that they provide variety, save time and are economical – at first seem self-evident. As for variety, we find that the number of items available in British supermarkets increased from about 1,500 in the 1950s to 15,000 in today's superstores. The increase is largely accounted for by convenience foods. In addition, sweet corn, peas, runner beans and broccoli, once highly seasonal, may now be bought in recognizable deep-frozen form, all year round. And (as I was told at a food technology meeting held in London's Royal Society in May 1974[62]) without such methods, people in large towns, or unfavourable climates, would be forever cut off from the joys of 'fresh' vegetables.

Close examination of this convenienced 'variety' shows all is not so simple. All cooks combine and permutate around a few ingredients. Fifteen combinations and permutations are possible from, say peas, carrots, turnips, and sweet corn. Different cooking methods extend the list towards infinity. The spectacular increase in 'variety' in the modern supermarket mainly results from combination, in the same packet or can, of things that a cook could have mixed himself in a few seconds: baked beans, baked beans with sausages, baked beans with pork, curried baked beans, baked beans with bacon, and so on. The difference is that a cook, given a free run of a modestly stocked larder, could extend the variety indefinitely.

In addition, we find items expensively packeted that were once sold without package. The Bramley cooking apple was adopted in Britain in the nineteenth century largely because it keeps so well: barring winds, it can be left on the tree until March – and that is before storage begins. It can now be bought, cut and pre-cooked, encased in aluminium and polythene. Another 'item' to swell the 'variety'. It still needs heating up; which, if you abandon the mania for peeling and coring (which takes only a few seconds even if you do not), is all the preparation the original needs.

And you are not supposed to select: the distributor selects for you. Scrabbling among the contents of the deep-freeze, to find the freshest, upsets the rotation. In Germany, packages of meat or what you will are presented, one at a time, on weight-sensitive shelves; you take, and the shelf is automatically replenished. An extreme example perhaps – but a logical extension. So much for choice.

The idea that deep-freeze increases the variety of available vegetables, in net, is simple deception. In practice only the market gardener, intercropping and catchcropping, harvesting each plant individually, can produce variety. Deep-freezing plants need bulk delivery – which requires vegetables to be grown by arable techniques. And arable farming – the big field, the big harvester – implies monoculture. Further, only a few species of vegetables freeze well; it is no accident, and has almost nothing to do with 'public demand', that half the frozen food sold in Britain is vegetable, and half the vegetables sold are peas. Peas stand up to arable growing techniques, and to the rigours of deep-freezing, particularly well.

Even here the field must be narrowed. Read any modern seed catalogue, and you find only a few of the many pea varieties marked as being suitable for deep-freezing. If you were growing on a farm, and not on a garden scale, the list would be even shorter: probably down to one. We suggested, too, in Chapter II, that the vegetables' chief asset – and peas, in this context are a 'green vegetable'; only when dried, and used in bulk, do they become a significant nutritional item – is flavour. The harvesting and freezing machines demand uniformity of size, appropriate resilience, and such irrelevancies as a long stalk on the pods. These qualities the breeders must bring out. Flavour is way down the list. Thus is the vegetable's *raison d'être* left out of account: we are not talking about gastronomy, but cosmetics.

In fruit – to digress slightly – we see an even more spectacular reduction in variety. At the end of the nineteenth century, more than 100 varieties of apples and 40 kinds of pears were regularly grown in British orchards. In apples, in commercial circles, Britain is now down to the Cox's, with Bramleys hanging on by the skin of their teeth. The beautiful old varieties – as different from one another as bananas are from pineapple – have gone by the board largely because of those very qualities that made them so desirable; their delicacy of flavour and flesh, their thinness of skin. They do not store. They do not keep. They do not take kindly to the wooden crate, and the journey by juggernaut.

What of seasonality? We have already suggested that a fundamental tenet of good cooking is to reflect the seasons. Why eat last month's peas when you could eat this month's broccoli and savoy? The aspiration is nonsensical. And the seasonality once gave rise to variety within each crop – as witness Jane Grigson's description of the mellowing haricot bean, in Provence. Peas too – varieties changing with the season; grading into mealiness towards autumn – once moved on with time. And vegetable seasons now seem so short largely because of the arable techniques required to produce them. Peas, even in Britain, and with-

out recourse to glass or polythene, can be produced five months of
the year: and if plant breeders were not busy lengthening the stalks,
they could lengthen the season still more. The deep-freeze factories
demand that the pea season lasts only a few hours, so that they can
sweep in and out with their combines. They solve the problems they
themselves create; they do not add to what was possible before.

What of locality? We are told that people in big towns could not
have fresh vegetables if it were not for the freezers. Ironically, the
reverse is true. Fresh vegetables in Britain (not all, but a lot) are first
sent to London for distribution. London, one of the biggest towns in
the world, is one of the few in Britain where you can guarantee to
buy fresh vegetables all year round. There is no technical problem.

What of people in unfavourable climates? All very well for the effete
southern Englanders to speak, but what of the wind-swept Scots?

Such cavils are born of ignorance. Here is Meg Dods, a great Scottish cook who has been compared to Mrs Beeton, and sometimes to
Brillat Savarin: 'Much has been done of late years to improve the
quality, to hasten the season, and to spread the cultivation of vegetables. Where a turnip, or a cabbage, or a leek was fifty years ago the
only vegetable luxury found on a country gentleman's table, we now
see a regular succession of not merely broccoli, cauliflower and peas,
but of the more recondite asparagus, seakale, endive, and artichoke,
with an abundance of early small saladings.

'The vegetable markets of most towns have within the same period
undergone a wonderful improvement . . . so that a healthful luxury
is now within the reach of all classes.'[63]

She wrote that in 1826. What Scotland could do without modern
pesticide and herbicide, without government advisers, without the
inroads of the post-Mendelian plant breeders, and in a time of con-
tinuing political unrest could be achieved ten times over in more favour-
able climes, in peacetime, with all the fabulous technique now
available. The only snag – as I have intimated, but will examine in more
detail – is that it is difficult to contain the necessary market gardens
and small retailers within the context of big business. Where is the
centralized production? Where the machines to eliminate labour?
Where the management and shareholders?

Even if we concede that the people of, say, Shetland or Alaska,
might be hard-pressed to produce variety in their long dark winters
(though that is a major concession; kale and a host of roots should
be available); and if we concede that people everywhere should have
access to good fresh vegetables; we still cannot justify the techno-

logical superstructures of the modern deep-freeze industry. It would be cheaper, if it was really thought worthwhile, to fly fresh vegetables daily by jet to the far-flung islands.

In short, the food industry's aspiration to present vegetables out of season and place contributes nothing to the cause of good gastronomy. Its claim to increase variety is in part a mathematical illusion, based on permutation and combination, while, because of its necessarily industrialized production, it is congenitally incapable of producing the vegetable varieties that could be provided by traditional methods. All we can say is that the processors are increasingly expropriating the means of production – so that in their absence, in the short term, there would be a vacuum. But it is a vacuum that could be filled, if the problem were merely technical, to superabundance.

What of convenience? On the micro-scale, we find the time saved in the kitchen largely illusory, and saved only at enormous expense. We have suggested that high tea, for day-to-day living, is more suitable for a working family than 'dinner', and that it is the ultimate convenience meal. 'Convenience' food is largely designed to produce a pastiche of dinner. But even here we find little saving. It takes less than a minute to peel a pound of potatoes, if you must peel them: and I costed the labour involved, when compared to the price of packeted 'mash', at £5 an hour at the rates of early 1975.

At the theoretical level, the illusion is obvious. To grow food and prepare meals from it requires a certain irreducible number of tasks. If the effort and time put into any one stage is reduced, then it must be taken up somewhere else along the line. And processing – introducing packages, additives, and the rest, where none are needed – increases the number of stages, and therefore the total magnitude of the task.

So we see a Birds Eye delegate addressing a meeting of the Royal Society in London, as follows: 'We have a splendid automated future planned for the cold store, but a word of warning is needed. Much of this growth depends on the growth of hypermarkets – and on their being situated well outside existing towns. At the moment not all town planners are convinced that the move away from the high street is a good one. But even if the large hypermarkets could be built in busy centres the legal restrictions on "juggernaut" type vehicles would limit the size of frozen food deliveries to such hypermarkets.'

Note that the 'splendid automated future' *depends* on the hypermarkets. Thus the price of a few minutes saved in the kitchen – minutes in which the potential pleasure of the kitchen arts is sacrificed to the splitting of polythene – requires an inversion of urban life; we save time (or think we do) yet to do so must travel miles by car. And as Gerald Leach records in *Energy and Food Production*, 'A survey in the USA has shown that from 1926 to 1968 weekly hours spent in food preparation dropped only from 23 to 18 while the time spent in "shipping and managerial tasks" rose from four to eight hours a week.'

And, of course, discussing 'convenience' we have wandered far from our original brief – to discuss methods of food production 'compatible with solving the world's food problems'. Who are we that we aspire to eschew all of life's necessary tasks? And do we really want to? Here is the Birds Eye delegate again at the Royal Society meeting: 'Today, 11 per cent of British homes have a home freezer . . . two million people have taken up . . . the latest "do-it-yourself" craze.' People, I suggest, do not want to be mere mouths, to be stoked by the food industry: people actually enjoy being involved in life's basic tasks, which after all are the basis of culture. The food industry knows this full well, and obligingly produces such things as 'take 'n bake' cake and bread mixes, which require the adding of eggs, for example, to create the illusion of work. Indeed, I have been told that it is a food industry ambition that people should come to regard its 'convenience' products merely as raw material for cooking, just as the industry regards wheat, beans, or what you will merely as raw materials for its own products. Thus have we gone full circle: but this time round, everything carries the expensive stamp of high technology. Expensive? What of the industry's claim to effect economies?

Bulk buying, bulk production, hard bargaining from a position of strength, the replacement of expensive labour by cheap fuelled machines – these are indeed the components of economy in a high riding country or commercial company; at least one that does not look too hard at the effects of its hard bargaining, or does not ask why the raw materials that it uses so profligately are cheap. But we have already seen in Chapter I, on the grand scale, how inappropriate are the food production methods of Britain and the US to the needs of the future world, when land must be used to best advantage, and fuel used sparingly and equitably. In the US and Britain, more than 50 per cent of all energy used in food production is used in processing.

On the small scale, the impression of economy is again largely illusory. Note that the fundamental commercial function of processing is to add value; to turn cheap raw material into something more expensive. Its function is analogous to that of over-emphatic meat production in agriculture. Packaged pre-cooked apples are not cheaper than fresh apples. Instant mash is not cheaper than potatoes. Deep-frozen strawberries may be cheaper than out-of-season fresh ones – but not cheaper than in-season blackberries or apples. If any commodity ever appears cheaper in its processed form, than in its fresh state – given that the fresh version is in season – then this is because the fresh are increasingly shuffled into inefficient markets. A rational agriculture needs correspondingly rational distribution; the products of market gardens do not fit neatly into the logic of the supermarket, which is built around the demands of mass manufacture. And the small greengrocer or butcher, shuffled into the side street, represents only the vestige of the traditional system. Where traditional markets flourish – in Brixton, Paris, Rome or Bangkok – the words variety and economy take on their proper meaning.

And the point made about convenience – that a task saved in one place is merely delegated elsewhere – applies equally to economy. The food industry aspires to strip itself of all unprofitable tasks. It does not bring the food to you: you go to the hypermarket. It will do only part of the storage: you need a deep-freeze to cope with its products. Who pays for your petrol? Who for the roads? Who pays for and houses your deep-freeze? All these items, and the time you take travelling to and from the hypermarket, are part of the total food bill. They do not appear on the company balance sheets. But they appear on yours, in the end.

But surely deep-freezing is merely an extension of storage techniques that are as old as – no, older than – agriculture itself? Surely storage is necessary? Why object simply because the systems have become more sophisticated?

Storage has two prime functions. The first is to guard against lean times. The second is to accommodate gluts that would otherwise be wasted.

To guard against lean times requires mass storage – and not of highly perishable commodities, such as green peas, but of items designed by nature to be stored: primarily the grains and beans. To defend the modern deep-freezing industry on the grounds that it is an aspect of the storage system that the World Food Conference agreed was so necessary is mere obfuscation.

And we have already conceded that freezing, or chilling, may reasonably be employed to cope with fish catches – and perhaps to store meat, killed when the summer pastures are spent. Gluts of vegetables and fruit, too, can reasonably be stored.

But the method here, is all important. The traditional way to store peas or beans was to dry them. Fruit was bottled, or turned into alcohol. Green vegetables were sometimes bottled or pickled – as in sauerkraut – or, as with green beans, laid down in salt. Traditionally, the storage methods were cheap. A farm or household invested only in a few jars. Because the investment was so low, these could be used only when there was glut. When there was not, they could reasonably be left out of service.

Invest in a home deep-freeze and you have to keep it permanently packed to justify the initial outlay and the running costs. Entire books are devoted to the logistics of making the freezer pay its way. You cannot merely store surplus. You must grow specifically in order to store. The same applies on the national scale: Birds Eye does not store the surplus pea crop, it employs farmers under contract specifically to keep the freeze-plants operative. There is no traditional precedent. Never before were gluts engineered to service the storage techniques. Tail is wagging the dog.

And of course, though some crops are highly seasonal, and though seasons vary, gluts are largely avoidable in a well-planned market garden. Peas, lettuces, and the rest were traditionally sown in rotation. Sprouts swelled their buds in sequence, over many weeks. Now the breeders strive to produce a sprout that will ripen all at once,[64] deliberately contriving the glut that the deep-freezers need, but which they pretend they try so hard to avoid. The problems so ingeniously solved are mostly of the industry's own making.

Nothing, then, contrived by the deep-freeze convenience food industry makes a worthwhile contribution to the necessary rational food system. Indeed, its erosion of traditional cooking and market gardening techniques, its squandering of energy and misuse of land, its confusion of issues and its diversion of talents – including that of the plant breeders – to increasingly trivial ends, serve to destroy the framework of skills on which a rational food system could be founded.

But if convenience food is mere frippery, the production of meat analogues from soya bean protein has been called 'one of the great food developments of all time'. That at least, was what Professor Aaron M. Altschul, of the School of Medicine in Georgetown University, was quoted as saying when Ranks Hovis McDougall launched their soya bean meat analogue, 'Protena', in Britain in June 1974.[65] Soya beans are not the only source of ersatz: Courtaulds were already marketing 'Kesp', made from field beans, which, unlike soya, grow well in Britain's temperate climate.

The rationale of ersatz meat production seems sound enough. You can produce more protein per acre from beans than from meat. But people like meat. So it seems reasonable, in the interests of world and national economy, to convert the vegetable into a passable imitation of the flesh.

And though aesthetes might object – Fay Maschler[66] is among British food writers who have greeted ersatz with suitable disdain – people adapt to the analogues well enough, once their 'prejudices' are overcome. In fact, present textured vegetable proteins are not intended totally to replace meat, but to 'extend' it: RHM recommend mixing Protena with meat in a ratio of up to 30:70. And in one test, 56 per cent of housewives preferred a 25:75 Protena–meat to an all meat hamburger. And, said the Protena literature, 'soya bean protein was introduced into the school meals programme by the US Department of Agriculture in 1971. In 1972–73 nearly 46 million pounds (20,838,000 kg) of soya protein, was used in school meals in the US and when used at the recommended levels in a meal it was usually chosen as "the preferred meal".'

On the individual scale, ersatz is cheap. Protena, after soaking, worked out (at mid-1974 prices) at eight or nine pence per pound. Meat at that time was at least three times that price. In short, ersatz will meet the nutritional needs and gastronomic aspirations of poorer people in an austere world. Objection is luddite, snobbish, elitist, and unrealistic.

Not all food experts outside industry wax quite as euphoric as Professor Altschul, but many condone the underlying logic of ersatz. Professor Kenneth Mellanby feels its development is inevitable: 'There are difficulties in processing (field beans) for animal food or meat analogues for human consumption. No doubt these difficulties will soon be overcome . . . there is little doubt that production and use (of meat analogues) will increase.'[67]

The Friends of the Earth, though often a thorn in industry's side, tell us in *Losing Ground*[68] that 'while developing countries seek to increase meat consumption, we may find ourselves seeking alternatives. Novel proteins may provide an answer . . . the economic impetus gained in America will be sufficient to carry the new products into the British market.

'At present the novel protein used for direct human consumption is derived from soya. Britain imported between 40,000 and 50,000 tonnes of soya protein, from America, in 1973. Research is under way to increase soya yields from their present acreage of 12 cwt (610 kg) per acre and to extend the geographical range within which soya can be grown.'

And here is Professor Yudkin, assuring us in his introduction to a symposium on meat held at Nottingham University in late 1974, that 'whatever way we adopt our consumption of traditional foods, we shall also need to eat quite new foods'.[69]

Let's be clear what we are talking about. The conversion of beans to ersatz does not increase their nutritional value; indeed, since oils and fibre are lost, the value is reduced. Ersatz could of course serve as a source of protein, but we have already seen that production of high-protein foods is no longer considered the prime desideratum – although it was when research into ersatz first got underway.

Today's hungry people are primarily in the Third World. All Third World cuisines already make extensive use of pulses, and of necessity have rarely made extensive use of meat. To suggest that it is better to use an expensive imitation of something they have never had in great quantity, rather than using the same thing in its original form as they have done for thousands of years, seems merely perverse. Ersatz cannot, and indeed is not intended to, contribute to the well-being of hungry people in the Third World. It is doubtful whether a commodity that cannot help those in most need can be considered one of the great food developments of all time.

But what of the west? Again, the idea that westerners need traditional high-protein supplements is ludicrous. Though there may be less meat in future, nobody need be short of protein as a result. There are protein-deficient people in the west – mostly among the old, and the children of the under-privileged – but their difficulties spring from chronic and deep-rooted social deprivation, and in the case of old people, from such obvious but incapacitating deficiences as lack of teeth, which lead them to a diet of bread-and-scrape and sweet tea. Another item on the already overladen supermarket shelves will not go to the roots of that problem.

We are down to gastronomy then; to the central dogma, repeated parrot-fashion by nutritionists across the western world, that people are driven to consume meat by innate carnivorous urges. We have seen that nothing, outside the growth economy which of necessity has pressed more and more meat onto the western market, supports this view. People in the 1950s and 1960s adapted to a high-meat diet: in the future, as throughout most of human history, they could, and without pressure would, adapt to relative meatlessness.

For we have seen that the great cuisines are based on sparing use of meat – frenetically 'extended', to borrow the technologists term, by potato, cereal, and the unprocessed bean. In the Cornish pasty, meat and potato, perhaps with turnip and carrot, and certainly with onion, is wrapped in pastry. The meat tricks out the potato and pastry protein: or, putting it another way, the pastry and potato 'extend' the meat protein. The meat and ersatz pie is not nutritionally superior: it may supply more protein, but the excess is superfluous and is wasted, since the body cannot store surfeit. Is the meat and ersatz pie gastronomically superior to the Cornish pasty?

That question should be rhetorical, but I have done a small experiment, at least as valid in its lack of controls as RHM's publicized study of 200 housewives. I made three meat loaves; one with meat 'extended' with ersatz; one including bread crumbs, with the same ratio to meat as the first; and the third containing potato. My long-suffering guests liked the second two. The first they nibbled nobly, but the bulk went to the chickens.

This of course exposes the false economy of ersatz. For its price should be compared not with meat, but with the perfectly acceptable beans from which it is made – or, more to the point, with potato or pastry that performs precisely the equivalent nutritional and gastronomic function in traditional cooking. Potatoes cost only three or four pence a pound in mid 1974.

Magnus Pyke, an influential nutritionist in Britain, has produced the theory that people, carnivores manqué, have an innate love of 'chewiness', which ersatz supplies and the original beans do not. Certainly, as a generalization, texture is important. But if people really 'demand' chewiness, why do meat producers strive so hard to produce 'tender' joints – and the packers sometimes squirt the carcasses full of protein-digesting enzymes? I have heard steak house managers say their fillets melt in the mouth, but never that they are 'chewy'. And why does the bread industry not extol the undoubted chewiness of wholemeal bread, which it resolutely refuses to market in worthwhile quantities? Why, indeed, does it emphasize the precisely opposite quality in its ultra-white 70 per cent loaves? In truth, to bring the discussion from the realms of fantasy, we may observe that the Italians, whose cuisine is largely founded on pasta in which 'bite' is all important, look for that elusive *al dente* resilience that is equally characteristic of unprocessed beans.

People could get to like ersatz: the Micky-Finning of school lunches is ensuring that the next generation gets off on the right foot. But what is the point? It is, of course, that if people do acquire a taste for ersatz, and if they are led to believe that its consumption is both economical and socially responsible, then they will be forever dependent on the good offices of the major food companies who are uniquely qualified to produce it.

As for the 'food experts' who apparently condone this industrial coup, I am inclined to believe what many cooks have long suspected; that they read a lot, write a lot, and talk too much, but never, ever, set foot inside a kitchen.

But whereas ersatz manufacture simply converts perfectly good food for which there are established cuisines into material of highly dubious appeal for which there is no precedent, the producers of yeast, fungus, bacterial, or algal protein, grown on industrial or agricultural waste or by-products, seem to be conjuring high-grade nutrient out of nothing. Here at least it seems that high technology is being turned to socially responsible ends. Yet all is not so simple.

The two processes that have made most progress are yeast production on oil by-products, and fungus production on agricultural waste or by-products.

The Birds Eye delegate at the Royal Society outlined the rationale of yeast protein production: 'Where a calf may double its weight in four weeks, a chicken in four days, a micro-organism can double its weight in four hours.' And of course the oil by-products – n-paraffins are the basis of British Petroleum and Liguichimica Biosenti's commercial yeast-protein processes – are produced in super-abundance in an industrialized world.

Objections. The oil by-products are not 'waste'; they command an appreciable market price. They are not used as yeast substrate as an alternative to throwing them away; but as an alternative to other processes. Yeast protein production is potentially dangerous. The cultures are easily contaminated with 'wild' and perhaps toxic strains. The substrate itself could be a contaminant; it contains carcinogens. And the protein, though high quality, does lack the essential amino acid methionine.

All these technical difficulties can be overcome. BP scientists are out of the top drawer. They can be relied upon to produce a pure, safe product. It would be absurd to impugn their ability or conscientiousness. But the difficulties can be overcome only at a price. Yeast protein cannot safely be produced on a tub of oil, stirred by a man with a stick. The techniques are subtler, more complex, more tightly controlled than in a modern brewery, where comparable problems are faced. Plants producing 100,000 tonnes a year by continuous culture

— such as the BP plant now established in Lavera, France — are considered appropriate to cover the costs. Capital cost of such a plant,
in mid 1975, was estimated at £20 to £30 million. In addition, despite the safeguards, 'single cell proteins' are not, and in the foreseeable future probably will not be, recommended for direct human
consumption. They are animal feed.

We thus have a process far too expensive for most Third World
countries to initiate themselves — but this is where the hungry people
are. And few would be able to afford to buy yeast protein produced
in the west — which would involve outbidding the US and Europe.
Even if they did so, they would be moving away from the ideal of self
reliance, putting themselves further into the debt of western nations,
which we have already identified as a major cause of their present
malaise.

And, of course, when the yeast proteins are fed to animals there is
an immediate protein loss of approximately 10 to 1. Hence the fabulous efficiency of the initial protein production is immediately squan-
dered. And such expensive feeds cannot reasonably be used except
in highly-controlled high-cost intensive livestock units, of the kind
that cannot be fitted into the framework of a rational agriculture.

Thus yeast proteins are far from being a world saver. At best they
will serve to prop up the profligate livestock industries of the west.
And that, if we are concerned with food production methods compatible with the needs of the whole world, is a futile and probably
pernicious ambition.

Some of these points were raised in an article in *New Scientist* by
Frazer Imrie,[70] who instead put the case for a Tate and Lyle project
to produce fungal protein on plantation waste in village scale plants in
Third World countries. At first sight the project seems eminently sensible. Imrie referred to a scheme in Belize (formerly British Honduras),
where fungi are grown on citrus waste to produce high-protein nutrient
appreciably more cheaply than could be imported. Such projects should
not be totally written off. As Imrie said, 'much land in developing
countries is unable to support human food crops even with the import-
ation of expensive fertilizers, herbicides, and pesticides. If this land
can be used to produce plant material which, through the mediation
of micro-organisms, will nurture animals for human food then an
advantage has been gained.'

But again we must tread carefully. We have shown that the prime
task for all Third World countries is, as outlined by the Chinese, to
strive for agricultural self reliance. Despite Imrie's point about 'land

unsuitable to support human crops', we find that the chief application of Tate and Lyle type projects is – as in Belize – to utilize plantation waste. After all, plenty of animals are adapted by nature to live in those wild areas where human food cannot be grown, without the benefit of fungal intermediaries. Yet we have already seen that a country that gears its agriculture to the plantation economy is putting itself in a highly precarious position. If it used the plantation land primarily to feed its own people then it would not have so much plantation waste. And if, after feeding its people, it had some room left for cash-crop plantations, it would not actually need to use the waste, since its people would already be fed.

Again, we find the process is chiefly designed to produce 'animal feed'. We have seen that in rational agriculture animals are used as sweepers, scavengers, exploiters of awkward ecological niches. The officious production of animal feed is useful only to supplement this scavenging role.

Here again, then, we find a technique whose prime function is to prop up a system that is fundamentally undesirable. In practice – though I cannot speak specifically for Belize – it could well be used to feed the minority who operate the plantation, and make no contribution to the mass who are not employed by the company. And we see that if integrated into a rational agriculture, this technique would be applicable only to supplement the diet of animals that could be produced in nutritionally and gastronomically adequate quantities anyway.

In short, no technological talisman can make good the deficiencies of misdirected agricultural policy. At best – or perhaps at worst – these sophisticated techniques may serve to obscure, for a time, the underlying faults. They may find a role in rational agricultures, but only a limited one; and they are worth considering only after the rational agriculture is established.

The Commercial Imperative

Why does the food industry behave the way it does? If wholemeal bread is nutritionally superior to white, and in many situations gastronomically superior, why do the bread magnates insist on promoting the 70 per cent loaf? If ersatz is a nonsense, why produce it? And why squander the chief merit of green vegetables – their flavour – simply to impose the rationale of deep-freezing?

The simple answer – 'to swell profits' – is true, but it smacks of 15-year-olds' cynicism. It implies what is not fundamentally true – that food manufacturers, as a race, are irresponsible sharks, out to make a quick buck and to hell with the consequences. Some may be. But many conversations with food technologists lead me to believe that precisely the opposite attitude prevails. Most people who study for diplomas and degrees in food technology, and beaver their lives away in the food industry, believe what they say; that they strive to bring the best possible food to the greatest number of people at the most economical price. And while people like me comfortably theorize and profitably scribble, the food technologists are out in the market place finding out what people want and trying to give it to them.

So let's not make this a personal battle. I concede for the most part that the technologists are highly motivated; that they see their relationship to society as that of the physician or guardian, rather than as that of the exploiter.

But let us not confuse the issue. The concession that most food technologists are well-meaning, and the observation that the major food companies do control a major part of western food production whether we like it or not, is directly responsible for the impotence of the various consumerist lobbies. Childish to write off the industrialists, say the consumerists; rather must we try to make sure, like an umpire seeing fair play, that industry is not led astray by its natural and venial exuberance: ensure, simply, that it does give us what we want.

Thus is the issue fudged. For the underlying capitalist logic of industrialized food production leads only incidentally to such obvious side effects as the over-use of additives and the promotion of ultra-white bread. Its chief fault is to lead us inexorably away from the necessary ideal of rational agriculture and cuisine. However well-meaning the industrialist, he is impelled, by the economic system of which he is a part, to do things totally opposite to what is required. Cynicism may be childish, but that central fact remains.

Food industrialists must make a profit. That is not cynicism. It does not imply that 'profit is a dirty word'. It is simply a fact.

The function of profit is not, primarily, in the modern world, to make management rich. Profit is one of several attributes of a healthy industry – necessary, above all, to attract investment, without which the industry founders. Indeed, since the food industry must advertise;[71] since it does plough much of its income back into plant and research; since it is – despite near or actual monopolies in several fields – highly competitive; and since selling is an uphill struggle because people are both conservative in their food habits, and have a limited capacity to consume, food is not the most obvious area for profiteering. The main economic strength of the food companies is that people must eat; and a food 'line', once established, should bring steady returns.

But without profit there is no investment: and in the quest for investment the food companies compete not simply with each other, but with all other industries in which people might put their money: with Fords, IBM, and the rest. So though food companies may only rarely make an overnight killing, as other innovators may do, they cannot afford simply to coast.

What must you do to make a profit? You must, of course, make the gap between selling price and costs as wide as possible. This has two aspects: first, reduce the costs; and second, add as much value as possible to the raw materials.

In a world where fuel has been cheap, and in which people's material aspirations are encouraged to be high, it tends to be cheaper to use machines than to employ lots of people who demand high wages. Hence it is cheaper to produce peas by arable methods – one man on a combine in a 50-acre (20 ha) field – than to raise them row by row. Land and energy are used profligately; but the biggest cost, labour, is reduced.

The machine is not used simply for preference. Its use is imperative. If you elect to produce peas by market garden techniques, and your rival uses the combine, then he will have the commercial edge. And the edge is all that is needed. If his peas sell one helfpenny cheaper than yours, or at the same price but with less cost, then his commercial health will inexorably increase at your expense. He will undermine your foundation as surely as a gentle tide will eventually erode a cliff. Hence voluntarily to adopt not to use the machine would be commercial suicide; it would be 'unrealistic'.

And the industrialist must use the cheapest possible materials. Admittedly, it sometimes pays, long term, to protect home agriculture. But if it is consistently cheaper to import African ground nuts than to grow beans at home, then African ground nuts must be imported. This may imply using underpaid African labour, and diverting the agriculture of a poor country from its essential task of feeding its own people. But the industrialist is a practical man doing a specific job. He was not directly responsible for establishing the imperialist relationship that makes such bargains possible. He must work within present constraints. To do otherwise is 'unrealistic'. By working according to the dictates of the system he of course reinforces it; but if society wants anything different, it is up to society at large to change the rules.

To increase returns, the manufacturer can both strive to increase consumption, and add value to the goods he sells. We have seen that to increase consumption of food is not as straightforward as to increase 'consumption' of cars, since people have a limited capacity to eat. But consumption can be increased indirectly – partly by selling non-nutritious comestibles, such as tea and coffee, and partly by channelling surplus through livestock. Hence, as we have seen in earlier chapters, increased meat production is a commercial imperative in a capitalist agriculture.

But the main source of increased return is added value: the raw material is converted into something ostensibly more 'desirable' and more expensive. Hence the biscuit becomes the chocolate biscuit, the chocolate biscuit acquires a layer of cream and a dollop of jam, and is sold in a see-through box; and beans, which could be sold by the half-hundredweight in paper sacks, are first converted into imitation meat, to sell by the pound at a price nicely adjusted to that of real meat.

But we saw in our discussion of rational agriculture that land must not be used profligately; and that energy cannot, except by perpetuating inequity, be sqandered in unnecessarily mechanized production, or in imposing gratuitous post-harvest processing. Yet it is commercially vital to use land and energy in this way. To attack the manufacturers for doing what they are forced to do is ridiculous, unless you simultaneously attack the commercial premises on which their activities are based.

But there is more to it than this. Machines do not simply replace labour; they impose a different logic. For one thing a machine, generally, is less versatile than a man. If a farmworker is not ploughing or harvesting – both highly seasonal jobs – then he can (on a mixed farm) be mending hedges or tending stock. A machine not fulfilling its predestined role simply depreciates. And machines are expensive. So once you mechanize you must – if you are to compete with others more alert than yourself – ensure the machines are used to full advantage.

We have seen a prime example of this in deep-freezing. Once the expensive plant is established the agricultural effort must be geared to its needs. The land is consequently mis-used because the necessary monoculture fails to make full use of it. Catch-cropping and inter-cropping techniques vital to full exploitation go by the board. But this becomes of secondary importance. Indeed, once one stage is mechanized, all the rest must adjust: as the Birds Eye delegate pointed out at the Royal Society: 'The splendid automated future depends on the growth of the hypermarket.' In practice, the commercially necessary reduction of agricultural labour affects the production strategy from the plant breeding stage to the moment the end product is dropped in the cooking pot.

More yet. Capitalism is about money – 'putting money to work'. The investor needs something to invest in. In a rational agriculture, based on thousands of overlapping small to medium sized farms and market gardens where is the possibility for investment? A rich man may own the land, but he is not then an investor – merely a landlord, who may, according to the best traditions, oversee the activities and welfare of the people who rent from him, or may, as is equally characteristic, simply take a cut. A rich man or a bank may put up the money for a smallholder to start work: but this is sponsorship, rather than investment. Capitalism is not mere neo-feudalism; it is not mere patronage; it is the investment of money in things with a definite value, and a predictable capacity to produce saleable commodities. The essential infrastructure of capitalism is the machine and the factory. Money, above all, is used efficiently; it must be centralized, accounted for, and ideally be sufficiently mobile to be shifted elsewhere if more profitable enterprises turn up.

Again, I am not saying capitalism is intrinsically evil. Even if this were true, that argument would be irrelevant. It is simply that the essential infrastructure of capitalism is totally different from that of rational agriculture. Rational agriculture is considered 'unrealistic' because it does not fit into the logic of our capitalist-based western society. The prime difficulties faced at the World Food Conference; the apparent recalcitrance of the US, which caused so many Third World hackles to rise;[72] the present absurdities of the EEC's Common Agricultural Policy, which demands that member countries should become more specialized and hence less able to exploit the land fully and use energy conservatively, spring directly from the capitalist necessity to impose the logic of industry onto agriculture. Indeed, politicians and farmers alike speak of British and US agriculture as being those countries' biggest 'industry'; as if the logic of manufacture could and should be imposed, willy nilly.

What of nutrition? The consumerists like to rap the industrialist over the knuckles for promoting foods, such as white bread or sweets, that are less nutritious than alternatives, or that are simply nutritionally pernicious. But again the industrialist has little choice. It is more profitable to promote the 70 per cent white loaf than the wholemeal; not least for the historical reason that present bakeries are geared to white loaf production, and it would be immensely expensive to change course. And people could eat wholemeal only at the expense of white bread: and because wholemeal requires less processing, it is a poor candidate for value-adding; and because it is bulky, people would tend to eat less of it than they can of white. Wholemeal is expensive at present, but only because it is produced on a small scale, and sold through highly specialist markets. But how can the industrialists bear the immense cost of changing their factories, or abandon their essential sidelines in the manufacture of animal feeds from bran and wheat germ, simply to provide a product that has less potential for profit than the present white loaf?

They cannot, of course. It would be commercial suicide. Which is why the pleas of consumerist lobbies that the giant bakers should change direction, are nonsensical. Unless you are prepared to dissect and reconstruct the entire economic structure of this major industry – with immense consequences for all related industries – then you are wasting everybody's time in demanding mass production and promotion of wholemeal bread.

So, too, with additives. Without preservatives, and anti-staling agents, and foaming agents, and artificial flavours and colours and the rest, food could not stand up to the rigours of manufacture, and the prolonged interval between harvest and sale, and appear looking fresh and fit for human consumption on the supermarket shelves. To attack the apparent 'over-use' of additives without attacking the economic logic that makes them necessary, is also nonsensical.

And, of course, the industrialists' claim that they will be able to adjust, if society did decide to curb profligate use of energy, or if energy prices simply became too high, is yet more nonsense. Take energy from industry, and industry collapses; and the economic logic that must strive to graft industrialization onto agriculture becomes inappropriate. Thus industrialized agriculture cannot adjust to austere use of energy. All that happens when energy is scarce is that the flaws in the fabric become more and more obvious – as in Britain, 1975. Food prices rocket and the products become more and more debased. The people are sold short, not because it is technically difficult to produce food, but because it is logically impossible to reconcile good conservative husbandry with machine-orientated agriculture. As I have stressed before, this argument is not an attack on the use of machines, a luddite plea for the scythe. But in a rational agriculture, machines are used to extend husbandry; in the US and Europe, they are used – and it is economically imperative that they are so used – to compensate for its absence.

Britain, in 1975, had a consumers' minister: Mrs Shirley Williams, a member of the Labour cabinet. She could fiddle about adjusting prices, putting on a subsidy here, or demanding price stabilization there. But (as she assured me in our one conversation) it was no part of her mandate to undermine the basic economic structure of a major industry. Britain has, after all, a 'mixed economy', and the Labour Party, no less than the Conservative, is pledged to uphold that mixture, as the left-wing are constantly reminded. But Mrs Williams's task was futile, as is any such minister's. Unless we re-lay the foundations, and build a food policy based in the logic of rational agriculture, then all else is arrows to the sun. It is not a question of painting the capitalist food producer as a black-hearted villain, it is just that he is congenitally incapable of doing what is needed.

But surely food industrialists can succeed only by doing what people want? Surely the underlying logic is not simply that of money and machine, but of democracy? We will examine this important argument in the next chapter.

Advocacy and Truth

The food industry argues that without its machinations, additives and all, we would all be poisoned more often, would have a less interesting diet, and would probably starve. This implies that the methods and logic of industrialized food production are alone capable of providing adequate food in a crowded world. As we have seen, the opposite is true. Certainly the overnight collapse of the food industry would cause chaos – not least because western agriculture, based on monoculture and contrived glut, is primarily geared to serve that industry. But this means only that the industry has pre-empted the means of production and distribution, so that alternatives have not been developed. It does not mean that present industrialization represents the best of all possible alternatives.

The industry's second defence, invoked to take the wind out of the sails of those who accuse it of anti-social behaviour, is that it can succeed only by doing what people want. This implies that the industry cannot flourish except by working within the confines of people's traditions and that the rapid expansion of the convenience food business, for example, could have occurred only in response to 'public demand'. Therefore, it seems, the industry is a democratic institution, providing a public service; and those who don't like it and what it does are romantics, elitists, or simple snobs.

This whole defence is based on half-truth and misinterpretation. Let's take expansion first. Certainly processed food sales have rocketed. As the Birds Eye delegate told the Royal Society meeting, Britons spent $1\frac{1}{2}$ per cent of their total food bill on frozen foods in 1962, and $2\frac{1}{2}$ per cent in 1972. And the US, as so often, provides a promise of things to come; for whereas Britons ate only 469,000 tonnes of frozen food in 1972, the American, with only four times as many people as Britain, ate six million tonnes.

Britain's rise in frozen foods is, said the Birds Eye delegate, a 'phenomenal growth'. But does it necessarily reflect 'demand'?

Just suppose, for argument's sake, that Britons in 1962 had no particular antipathy to frozen peas. People like peas, after all, and tinned peas had established the precedent for processing. Suppose the people were just as fond of frozen peas as of, say, cabbage. Then their chances of buying frozen peas or cabbage on any one visit to the supermarket would be evens – 50/50.

But suppose the peas were slightly more prominent than the cabbages. Suppose they occupied a lighted display cabinet, while the cabbage was put at the back of the store. There is no 'suppose' about it, in fact: a storekeeper must draw attention to his frozen food cabinet to cover its capital and running costs, and because its value-added contents are potentially more profitable than fresh vegetables.[73] But if the peas are slightly better laid out than the cabbage, then the customer's chances of buying them increase, ever so slightly, from 50 per cent to, say, 50·0001 per cent. That figure is, of course, hypothetical. The point is that increased availability alone will improve people's chances of buying a particular commodity ever so slightly; and companies with the wealth of Unilever behind them, and a strong influence over the supermarket outlets, can afford to make their products more readily available; and to increase the chances of any one person buying a particular commodity on any one occasion will, over a decade and a population, produce the kind of 'phenomenal growth' that has been seen in Britain. No specific 'public demand' for frozen peas need be supposed; merely a slight tipping of balance in favour of their being bought.

Nonetheless, Birds Eye can sell its frozen peas only because people like peas. To sell what people like is to work within the confines of established tradition. Indeed, food companies cannot move outside tradition; which is another way of saying they must give people what people want.

But food 'traditions', though perhaps conservative, are, above all, heterogeneous. Within a single family – as a recent advertisement for a certain Birds Eye pie reminded us – tastes vary tremendously. Across a whole society a thousand different tastes and predilections – and myths and prejudices – can be found. To work within tradition, the food industry has merely to emphasize, from among the vast range of possibilities, those 'lines' that are most acceptable to value-adding processing. People like peas, of course. But they also like cabbage, sprouts, and cauliflower. Peas are the mainstay of Birds Eye's deep-frozen vegetable enterprise not because people rank them above all else, but because they are easily farmed by arable technique and stand up to deep-freezing.

The same argument applies to white bread sales. At least since Roman times people have been prepared to pay more for white bread. There are many reasons for this. Roman wheat grains, after all, were not so nicely swollen as the modern strains; the proportion of bran must have been far higher, and the resultant bread gritty. But primarily, the desire for whiteness had to do with social status. Peasants were brown, because they worked in the fields. Barbarians were brown. Dark colour has been associated with dirt, graft, and general coarseness until well into this century. In addition, white bread, which requires more processing, used to be dearer than brown or black – and hence was the prerogative of the rich. The ancient predilection for white bread had some roots in gastronomy; but its origins were mainly social.

Today the myth is, if anything, reversed. Brown, sun-tanned skin is associated not with graft and poverty, but with health, leisure, and wealth. Black is beautiful. In Britain (though not in the US) brown eggs carry a premium. The food industry could, if it chose, cash in on the modern brown-is-healthy myth, and market a wholemeal bread that really was nutritionally superior to the 70 per cent white. Expensive specialist brown (but not wholemeal) loaves, such as 'Hovis', are indeed sold on the basis of the brown equals 'country goodness' myth. But we have seen that to promote wholemeal bread would be commercially absurd. Therefore the industry chooses to perpetuate the white equals purity myth, and ignore the equally strong brown equals health myth. Food myths, as well as traditions, cover a wide spectrum. But to emphasize those most commercially suitable is not the same as meeting public demand. That would imply responding to the complete spectrum.

When it chooses, the industry takes pains to obliterate myth. Thus TVP (Textured Vegetable Protein) at first suffered from the prejudice against 'artificial' food. Ersatz meat made from fungus is liable to suffer even more[74] from the popular association of fungi with mouldiness – though mushrooms and truffles are highly esteemed, as are Roquefort, Stilton, and Gorgonzola. In general, as the Birds Eye delegate told the Royal Society: 'The work of the food scientist is probably as misunderstood today as Galileo's revelation to his contemporaries that the world was indeed not flat . . . tell (the public) that any part of (their food) has been touched by science and you will probably confirm their worst suspicions about the unspeakable chemicals the food industry is putting into their steak and kidney pie and peas . . . we have indeed a communications gap of gargantuan proportions between the food scientists and the public.'

I believe – despite the amazingly conceited analogy with Galileo – that this is true, and insofar as the 'communications gap' springs from ignorance, rather than informed insight, it is regrettable. But note that

there is no suggestion here of acting out people's desires, or of working within the context of established myth. The communications gap,
we are constantly reminded, must be bridged by 'public education'. In
short, the food industry will cash in on those aspects of tradition,
prejudice, myth, or what you will, that suit its techniques: but will
work extremely hard to obliterate any psychological barriers to its
progress. It does not, and cannot, simply give 'the public' what 'it'
demands. Industry can do only what industry can do.

And despite our alleged conservatism, history demonstrates how
quickly tradition can be changed. Tea, coffee, and chocolate became
established in Europe in a few decades. Canned foods dates only from
the last century. This century saw cornflakes all but obliterate breakfast
porridge. Convenience and deep-frozen foods took off after the second
World War. To alter the tradition or establish a new one, the processor both emphasizes the advantages of his new products, and – as
with frozen display cabinets – makes them constantly and clamour-
ously available. At the same time he subtly denigrates the traditional
fare.

Both approaches are seen in impressive action in many Third World
countries, where bottle feeding in a few years has largely replaced
breast feeding – though breast feeding is a tradition as old as mankind,
and as deeply rooted as a tradition can be. [75, 76]

In Ibadan, Nigeria, a study showed that more than 70 per cent of
mothers now begin bottle feeding before their babies are four months
old – though breast feeding was traditionally continued for four years.
In Chile 20 years ago, 95 per cent of children were breast fed for at
least a year; now only 20 per cent are breast fed for two months.

The consequences, now widely catalogued, are evil. Cost is one snag.
A Nigerian woman could provide herself with enough extra local food
for adequate lactation, for 21p a week. Using the cheapest kind of
artificial feeds – modified skimmed milk powders – the cost would be
32p in foreign exchange. Commercially available infant milks, used
instead of breast milk, would cost £1.15 per week. Feeding a six-
month-old baby can take half the Nigerian family's income. Consequently the mothers – whose breasts rapidly dry up for want of suck-
ling – are obliged to dilute the feed. So the babies are inadequately
fed.

Hygiene is the second chief bugbear. A Cow and Gate Babycare
Booklet for West Africa tells mothers to 'place bottle and lid in sauce-
pan with sufficient water to cover them', and to 'bring to the boil and
allow to boil for 10 minutes'. But as Dr David Morley, of the Institute

of Child Health in London, has pointed out,[75] the standard stove in West African villages is the 'three stone kitchen' – a pot supported by three stones above a wood fire. It could take an hour or two to bring the water to the boil on such a stove, and – with no cold water on tap – another hour to cool down. So the mothers do not boil; they cannot sterilize the bottles. To the baby's inadequate feed, therefore, is added the burden of infection. Breast milk needs no sterilization.

Bottle feeding is not, of course, entirely responsible for the increasing tally of marasmus and infant death in the Third World. But a WHO bulletin published in 1973 reported that Chilean babies bottle fed in the first three months had three times the mortality rate of their brothers and sisters who were exclusively breast fed, and detailed research in Jamaica, India, and Arab communities in Israel has produced comparable findings.

The baby milk manufacturers say their products are necessary because some mothers cannot lactate. Yet in one study Dr Morley found that fewer than 1 per cent of mothers in a Nigerian village had serious breast feeding problems, and though 2 or 3 per cent had temporary trouble due to illness they still managed to breast feed for most of the first six months.

The baby milks sell not because they are necessary or advantageous – how can they be when the babies die before their mothers' eyes? – but because they are sold, sold, and sold again. Big bouncing babies on hoardings represent the prize of bottle feeding. The emotive word 'protein' is bandied: the fact that the cow's milk on which the baby milks are based is richer in protein because calves naturally grow fast and humans do not is not mentioned. The enviable middle class can be seen to have abandoned breast feeding – so breast feeding is primitive. Company representatives dressed as nurses appear in clinics and hospitals, presenting, in the words of one report, a 'sales pitch in the guise of nutritional advice'. The baby food companies ply the maternity hospitals with free milk samples. Only the feed required throughout the following year has to be bought.

I have outlined the baby milk story not to appeal to your emotions, but to illustrate how wide can be the gap between a food company's stated intention, and the actual consequences of its action; how inevitable and inexorable is the commercial process; how easily an unsophisticated and insecure people can be led; but, above all, to show how frangible are the traditions that are supposed to guard humanity from sales pressure.

Westerners are far from being immune. The magic word 'protein' is still used to sell baby foods. I have sat in the company of food industry promoters while they discussed the possibility of marketing ice cream on the basis of its protein content; they would not, of course, point out that protein bought in such a form is extremely expensive, or that protein accompanied by so many calories is too dilute by half.

And the word 'calories', used disparagingly when industry wants to sell a new 'slimming' loaf – fewer calories per slice because the slices are thin and have holes in – crops up as 'energy', when industry finds itself with a high-carbohydrate product. Hence cornflakes, a current British TV advertisement assures us, send children radiantly to school. That an identical energy source – cereal starch – is available in bread at a fraction the cost is not mentioned. So too is the magic word 'vitamins' used to push new products – as we have seen in Chapter VIII.

In short, the argument that increased food sales reflect public demand is only half true. The idea that the food industry can operate only within the confines of tradition is also only half true, and if true, would be trivial. And the idea that tradition's confines are inflexible and cannot be expanded by sales pressure, is, as recent history in the Third World and the west demonstrates, ludicrous.

But the industrialists have yet another line of defence. We cannot tell people what to do, they say. We can only present information. The public is free to judge that information – just as a high-court judge can assess the advocacy of counsel. And, to extend the analogy, the public, like the judge, has the final say. To suggest that people need protection from industrial advocacy is to insult their intelligence.

The idea that industry can promote its goods only by advocacy is not true, as we have seen; it can to a large extent determine what is available to be bought. And the idea that people at large can judge its advocacy, as a high court judge judges counsel; the implication that commerce is constrained in the real world, as lawyers are in a court of law, is far from being the whole truth.

Note, first, that although learned counsels do not lie in a court of law, they do not put their opponent's case either. What the defence counsel says is true, but only as far as it goes. 'Truth', for forensic purposes, is supposed to lie between the case for the defence and that of the prosecution.

In real life, in the case of the food industry, we never hear the advocacy for the prosecution. We hear voices raised in protest, from consumerist or health-food lobbies, or market gardeners squeezed out of business; but most of the protestors have missed much of the point, the groups do not cohere, and individually they have neither the power nor the wealth to bring their case before the public; and in practice their arguments are presented primarily in arcane publications read only by those already convinced. To get together the case for the prosecution in this book has required beavering among papers, journals, and lectures that most people never got to and which were not reported in the front-line press.

What of the public's 'freedom' to judge the industry's advocacy? Note, first, that the judge does not pass judgment until he has heard both sides. The public hears only one side. Note, also, that the judge is the best informed person in court. He can see what parts of the counsel's presentation are germane, and what is mere rhetoric. And he has the power to direct the advocates, if they imply more than they say. To suggest that people at large are not able to judge what the food industry tells them is not to insult their intelligence. It means merely that most people are not food specialists; that they hear only one side of the argument; and that most people do not actually expect to be deceived, and so are unprepared. It takes a certain deviousness of mind to see that a slimming loaf is slimming because it is full of fresh air.

But surely the public is protected. The US has its Food and Drug Administration, and Britain has various safety committees, to ensure that food products are not actually harmful. Advertisers' own ethical committees ensure that advertisements do not lie.

Still, to continue our analogy, we have nothing comparable to the counsel for the prosecution. The task of the FDA is not to provide people with alternatives to industrial products, merely to see that the only 'alternative' proferred is not immediately dangerous. The advertising ethical committees are comparable to the law societies: their function is merely to see that the lawyers are not bent.

If the food industry's advocacy were to be as fair as that of the counsel for defence – and we would still be lacking a judge – it would have to be constantly opposed by equal and opposite counter-advocacy. An advertisement telling you that frozen peas contained more vitamin C than tinned peas, should be followed by, 'yes, but fresh broccoli, now in season, contains more still; and peas in any case do not contribute significantly to your vitamin C balance; and the vitamin C in potatoes is cheaper'. A hoarding that said Blogg's baby food was rich in protein would be countered by one saying, 'yes, but babies do not need a high protein concentration; and some evidence suggests that excess may lead to too-rapid growth, in turn laying the foundations for obesity in later life'.[36] And advertisements telling you how much time you save buying instant mash would have voices over to point out that the time saved should be costed at £5 an hour, and that the product is nutritionally inferior to the real thing. And advertisements urging us to 'buy a bigger piece' of meat, might, *inter alia*, illustrate the Third World suffering at the other end of the line.

But advocacy breeds advocacy, as any one who has been to law knows. The expense of argument-counterargument would in the end be met by the consumers. Food needs no advocacy: people must eat; they will buy food without Unilever's prompting. In short, it would be better not to advertise food at all. Indeed, since the most advertised products are the value-added ones, most liable to increase food bills, and requiring profligate use of energy and land, it is far more pernicious to advertise food than to advertise cigarettes. It is typical of our society, with a fondness for grand gestures that leave the basic structures intact to condemn the second and leave the first with virtually a clear field.

I would like to end this chapter here – with the comforting thought that food industry advocacy ends with food industry advertisements. But, of course, it does not. Many academics in high places agree with the general thesis of this book, or with many aspects of it: I would not have had the confidence to write it otherwise. But their voices are not the ones you hear: the academics heard in the most widely reported public meetings, or most widely circulated literature, are those who condone industrial techniques. The reason is fairly obvious. Publications and meetings cost money; and industry can supply it.

I am not implying corruption. The voice of industry rises above the rest as by Darwinian natural selection; the most robust inevitably dominates. Thus in an anonymous editorial in the *Lancet*,[77] as far back as 1972, we find a biochemist from University College Hospital, London, putting a strong nutritional and social case against ersatz meat made from beans. The opinion mailed direct to the front-line press in Britain when Protena was launched in 1974 was that of Professor Altschul – that soya steak is one of the great breakthroughs of all time. The Royal Society was founded in the seventeenth century as a forum for unfettered intelligence; what is spoken within its walls is hallowed. Yet in 1974 at the meeting on food technology I have referred to, – one of the very few in its 300-year history concerned with day-to-day practical affairs – none of the obvious objections to modern practices were voiced, and none of the alternatives mooted. The Society was used simply as an industrial showcase, and nobody seemed to mind.

Many university nutrition departments rely heavily on industry for finance. Again, the question of corruption does not arise; I believe the charge would be absurd. But the idea is fostered that only industry, which has the power to effect change, is capable of producing viable food policies; that the only techniques and rationale that are 'realistic' are those of industry. And, of course, the techniques of industry are those of high technology. The scientists' raison d'être is to seek technological solution. Only a few, some of whom are acknowledged at the beginning of this book, have the humility and vision to ask whether the most mechanized and spectacular solution is necessarily the appropriate one.

At the school level we find – to judge from my discussions with Britain's Association for Science Education – teachers anxious to give their pupils as broad a view as possible. Yet the information available to them to pass on, comes largely from the food industry: a British Nutrition Foundation *Bulletin* lists 18 teaching aids for schools,[80] 13 supplied by commercial organizations. The information is not mere propaganda. But it helps create the general impression that food supply is the prerogative of the established food industry. With that premise founded, the details can follow.

And, of course, we find textured vegetable proteins introduced into the US School Feeding Programme – which 'introduced 25 million children in 80,000 schools to the idea of substitute meats' – and Britain, now, following suit. We find discussion of 'unconventional protein sources' written into high-school social science syllabuses. We also find 'domestic science' lessons instructing in the use of convenience foods. We rarely find lessons in gardening or animal husbandry, or on cooking things straight from the ground.

In short, the only coherent and consistent voice is industry's. The belief is being fostered in the next generation that survival itself depends on the good offices of industry. The techniques that could reveal the nonsense of this are neglected or put forward by specialist lobbies – the vegetarians, self-sufficers and the like – who do not cohere one with another, and who do not, individually, provide a viable alternative.

Food industrialists – and their satellite academics – are apt to tell us that what we lack is 'education'. If only we were not prejudiced and old fashioned, if only we did not react to the food scientist as the inquisition did to Galileo, then we would see how beneficently the industry strives on our behalf. But the advocacy we are subjected to, incoherently countered and virtually unfettered, is not the stuff of education, but of indoctrination – almost the precise opposite. Nothing would do this industry more harm than an education that led to understanding.

The Way Ahead

Some will have read the chapter on rational agriculture, the pivot of this book, and winced. On the one hand, these critics will suggest, I seem to be throwing away science and technology. Yet science has brought great benefits; there is no reason to suppose that the inventive spring will dry up; and only a member of the effete middle class could deny, or apparently deny, the value of machines that save labour. If the author's back had never been broken by graft, he would soon change his argument.

Secondly, I hear the critics shout, the rational agriculture demands a degree of central organization quite unacceptable in a western democracy. What of freedom? What of a man's right to aspire to excel himself – or his fellow men, if he has the talent? Certainly the rational agriculture might succeed technically – but as much could be said about a colony of ants. And we have seen, in our own century and many times in centuries past, human beings reduced to the level of the ant. Have we struggled for three thousand years to hammer out a society in which people can walk abroad without fear on the one hand, and can express themselves on the other, just to throw it away at the first sign of danger? Certainly the world is in a parlous state – and whenever danger threatens, extremism, whether left wing or right, raises its ugly head. But a little patience is all that is required; neither visions of utopia, nor of repulsive regimentation, are called for. Not only is the 'rational agriculture' unrealistic: the price of it is far too high.

These are obvious and serious charges, and they deserve serious answer.

Firstly, I think, we should re-stress the seriousness and uniqueness of the present world food situation. Many societies in the past – in sixteenth-century England; or fourth-century Rome – have believed that their societies had outgrown their resource. In truth they had merely come up against the limitations of their agricultural techniques – or, more accurately, against the limitations of the policies that those techniques subserved. To some exent the present world food situation is similar. We have not exceeded physical capacity, but have merely begun to expose the flaws in policies not designed to feed all the people.

But now, as has never been true before – even though our ancestors may on occasion have believed it to be true – we know we are within sight of the limits of our resources. We must, if we want to survive other than by periodically obliterating half the human race, operate more conservatively than was ever necessary before. We are up against a new imperative, and we cannot assume that all our conceits and techniques that carried us through before, will work in this uniquely different situation. Of course we need not, and should not, sacrifice all the good things that we have strived for. But we must re-think.

We could add, in passing, that the solutions adopted by our fore-fathers to solve their superficially similar production problems are not acceptable. European expansion in the seventeenth, eighteenth, and nineteenth centuries was achieved only by obliterating the red man in the Americas and the black man in Australia, by decimating the black man in Africa,[81] and subjugating almost the whole of Asia. We have not only to re-think our production techniques, but also to re-think our political ethics.

Now for the specific criticisms of rational food production. It would, of course, be absurd to deny the benefits of science and technology. Tractors can do things that horses cannot, and combine harvesters can bring in a crop in a few brief hours of sunshine in a wet autumn, while armies of men with scythes would stand helplessly by. And though modern tractor drivers suffer – the noise in the safety cab can be as high as in a steelworks, and the vibration causes osteoarthritis in the spine – I would rather drive a tractor than swing a blade.

But it is not true that machines can totally obviate the need for physical work. For example, we have seen from the discussion of energy in Chapter I, that to a large extent the hard-pressed farm labourer has simply been replaced by the production line shift worker, making the machinery. To aspire to eliminate all physical work is non-sensical, not only because it is theoretically impossible, but also be-cause, in striving to replace man by machine, we automatically use energy and land profligately – both of which are incompatible with the world's present needs. In addition, the idea that people in general aspire to do no work is an absurd piece of cynicism. Coalminers, in their time off, do not simply sit around, they grow vegetables, sing and race pigeons. 'Do-it-yourself', and, now, self-sufficiency, are grow-ing apace among the western middle class – not simply to save money, but because working at tasks with a discernible end product is satis-fying. More generally, nothing is more soul-destroying than unemploy-ment.

Agricultural work can be hard; often the hardship can be relieved by machine. But the hardship of farmworkers in previous centuries did not spring from lack of mechanization, but primarily from exploitation. In the novels of Thomas Hardy, who knew of what he wrote, the seasonal graft of harvest depicted in *Far from the Madding Crowd* is hard but satisfying. Only in episodes in *Tess of the d'Urbervilles* does work take on the deadening aspect of slavery – because, in those episodes, the workers were indeed employed as serfs.

And though machines have driven many people from the land in Britain and the US, they have not always made life easier for those who are left. Modern intensive pig and poultry units have a high labour turnover precisely because the job, though perhaps requiring little muscle power, is physically and mentally so debilitating. The modern dairyman, tending 70 or more cows to a split-second, is under at least as great a pressure as his equivalent of 30 or 100 years ago. Mortality and morbidity among today's farm workers ranks with those of coalminers, building workers, and deep-sea fishermen.[82]

Insofar as the lot of farm workers has improved in Britain and the US in this century – and improvement has certainly not been commensurate with that of the rest of society – it is political and social change (often vigorously opposed) that have been mainly responsible. And it is political and social change, rather than further mechanization, that could bring about further improvement.

And what has mechanization achieved in western agriculture? Certainly productivity has increased this century – in parallel with the increase in mechanization and manufactured fertilizer. But we saw in Chapter I that in Britain, which provides a useful object lesson for the rest of the world because its progress is so well documented, yield per useable acre has increased only one and a half times. The increase in yield falls short of the increase in energy use by an order of magnitude. In truth the chief function of mechanization, its raison d'être, has been to replace husbandry. Instead of comparing output now with that at the turn of the century – a chastening enough comparison – we should compare it with what it could be, if mechanization and industrial chemistry had instead been used to extend the effectiveness of the husbandman. The study cited in Chapter I – showing that amateurs using only 14 per cent of the total area produced as much, in cash terms, as modern agriculture using the whole – gives a clue to what might have been. Let's not deny the value of machine and science; but we should acknowledge that its present role, to replace husbandry by something else – 'agribusiness' is the appropriately ugly word – is a gross mis-use.

And we are not talking simply about machinery. While Britain and probably the US throw away a quarter of their food, almost all of it suitable for chickens, scientists strive to increase the growth rate of deep-litter broilers, fed largely on grain that humans could eat, by fractions of a per cent. Because the margin for improvement is now so small, the research seems impressively precise. Huge numbers of birds are required to produce results whose validity can be assessed only by the use of arcane statistics. Yet the problem the scientists so intricately and expensively strive to solve results directly from the ineptitude of the underlying agricultural strategy. This is the complexity that conceals artlessness.

We should, as has never been done in the west, clearly define the problem that agriculture should solve: then work out the necessary infrastructure, the apportionment of land and the regional distribution of crops best suited to meet that aspiration; and then work out how machines, chemistry, and breeding, can best contribute. Only then will we be able to select the appropriate technology.

But an oft-voiced criticism is that technology is all one. All very well to work out that we need tractors of a given size, or a digester for producing methane fuel from pig effluent, but such things are not produced out of thin air. Modern tractors grew out of a broad-based motor industry, borrowing techniques from car and aircraft engine. The methane producer has a long and convoluted pedigree, involving high-flying chemistry and engineering originally conceived for totally different purposes. Either you decide to mechanize or you don't. If you simply pick out these, and these, and these machines, you destroy the industries and disciplines that are alone capable of producing them.

There are two separate aspects of this criticism. First, we must concede that technology benefits from a broad base. The aircraft industry in particular, with its obsession for reducing weight and maximizing strength, and its study of wind flow and drag, has had far reaching effects in building design, and, for example, medical instrumentation. If we decided for some reason that aeroplanes were not desirable, then we would automatically sacrifice the side benefits.

But this argument can be, and has been, overstated. Thus the US space programme has sometimes been justified on the grounds of 'spin-off'. Yet its only discernible contributions to day-to-day living are the space blanket (used by mountaineers and occasionally by midwives to wrap premature babies) and the non-stick frying pan.[83]

In addition, technology has pre-emptive as well as synergistic effects. The concentration on the internal combustion engine has precluded advances in other fields – of stirling engines, or linear motors, for example.

In short, by concentrating effort on producing specific machines with circumscribed functions, we would lose out on the spin-off we might have got from allowing other projects to flourish. But we would also gain by concentration of effort. The tractor may have benefited from the automobile; but it is nonsensical to argue that we need the complete spectrum of western vehicle production in order to produce satisfactory tractors.

Second, it is true that the Ford tractor, for example, is produced by a company that has made most of its money producing cars; and possible that without those cars there would be no Ford tractors, because there would be insufficient finance. The only point here, though, is that it is the money and not the technology, that is homogenous. Thus Geoffrey Rippon has been known to justify production of Concorde, on the grounds that it will make money, without which Britain would be unable to do useful things. Even if this were not demonstrably untrue (since Concorde is bound to lose money), the idea that we should continue to do totally unnecessary things, in order to make enough money to do necessary things, is inappropriate in a world that can no longer afford to squander effort and resource.

Historically, of course, technology – from the end of the eighteenth century – has grown hand in hand with capitalism. To put it crudely, capitalism provided the money to finance the technology, and technology the means to make the money into more money, which could then be fed back to advance the technology, and so on. And technology makes possible the centralization that is the essence of capitalism. Hence the two, in western societies, seem ineluctably yoked. Hence is seems that if we upset capitalism (as rational agriculture would do) then we automatically kill the goose that lays the technological eggs that alone could make the rational agriculture work.

In truth, of course, technology can grow in non-capitalist countries, as it has in modern Russia and China. More to the point, the only technology that is developed by capitalism is that which serves the ends of capitalism. Hence rational agriculture would probably make extensive use of 'intermediate technology' – windmills, digesters, and the rest. Capitalism has not produced such devices (except on the small scale to meet the aspirations of a few eccentric, and generally fairly well-heeled, self-sufficers) precisely because they are the machines of de-centralization. They do not tend to bring people together into factories; rather do they tend to keep them apart, in diffuse societies that provide no levers for investment. In short we not only find that capitalism does not provide a suitable economic base for rational agriculture, but that it is also incapable of providing appropriate technology. We must see that the conceptual link between technology and capitalism is in truth only an historical one, peculiar to the west, and that the link can and must be severed.

It is also argued that mechanization represents some kind of spiritual advance; not simply in freeing people from hard labour, which it can do only if properly applied, but because it represents the advance of science, and science represents intellectual advance. To curb technological progress is (according to this argument) an act of philistinism, comparable with telling artists what to paint, as in Russia, or condemning Beethoven as a bourgeois lackey, as has been known to happen in China.

And to slow the march of science by curbing technology is not only philistine, but perilous. After all, the advance of western society has depended largely upon scientific leaps into the unknown, by brave and brilliant men, sometimes feared by their contemporaries (as was Galileo) and sometimes derided (like the Wright brothers). To say enough is enough is to act with the same stultifying conservatism as the Inquisition.

This is a beguiling argument. Scientists have pulled many rabbits from hats, and presumably could continue to do so, and the kind of agrarian shuffle proposed in this book would be inhibiting. But the argument is also muddle headed.

First, I suggest that science is both a cultural indulgence, that gives gifted intellectuals a high, and is a means of effecting change: a political weapon. As a cultural indulgence it is unique; it has ways of putting its truths to the test, by experiment, that other indulgences, such as theology, do not. Art 'advances' in a sense, as techniques are refined and constraints (such as the musical diatonic scale) are broken. But only science can constantly match its ideas and observations against the unchangeable fact of the real world; only in science can the evolution truly be said to be directional.

That said, however, I do not believe that science, as a cultural indulgence, should be ranked above any other. There is no particular reason why society should give scientists carte blanche to indulge their fancies, rather than, say, musicians, carpenters, or gymnasts.

The only reason why society might strive officiously to accommodate scientists is if those scientists produce things to its benefit. If, indeed, the scientists do not merely play with ideas, as a bridge player might, but do demonstrably useful things. But we have gone well beyond the stage when mere mechanization, or the substitution of artificial fertilizer for old fashioned dung, can be automatically considered an improvement. We now have abundant evidence – another reason why our present food problem is different from that of all previous societies – that technology inappropriately applied can not only have gruesome side effects, but can frustrate the ends for which it was originally conceived. Ivan Illich has emphasized this point with respect, *inter alia*, to transport.[84] In agriculture we have seen that to gear monocultural production to the needs of the ever-enlarging combine is to abandon the subtleties of husbandry that alone could consistently increase production.

Indeed I suggest – as is already becoming widely accepted in western medicine, which has a longer scientific pedigree than agriculture – that the most sophisticated stance is not to rank science and its wonder toys above every alternative, but to be able to select from it what serves useful ends and what does not. We can draw a parellel with painters, who do not use more colours as their sophistication grows, but learn to select the minimum that will express their ideas; or with great writers, who do not lard their prose with every fine phrase they can think of, but eliminate everything, no matter how spectacular, that does not contribute. We have allowed our technique to run away with us, like a 15-year-old poet.[85] Our open-eyed wonderment at the marvels of science: that *is* philistinism.

In truth the west has never come to terms with its intellectuals in general, and with its scientists in particular. In principle, the dilemma is simple. Without intellectuals – in the broad sense, of people who can think deeply and originally, and in the narrower sense, of people who are 'expert' – a society cannot advance. But because the intellectual, or expert, can do things that the 'layman' cannot; and because – as when a sick man needs a doctor – the layman may at times need the ministrations of the expert, the expert has power. And because the layman does not understand how the expert works, or what he does, he must trust the expert.

Socrates argues, in Plato's *Republic*, that because the expert has power over the layman, that he also has a right to power; in other words, that the 'just' society is one in which the difficult things are done by an intellectual elite, who should also be, by virtue of their expertise, the ruling class. This, as has often been pointed out (not least by the American psychiatrist, Thomas Szasz)[86] is the rubric of fascism.

In the modern west, the actual power that experts have by virtue of their expertise is given spiritual connotations. It is written into our concept of democracy – perhaps, indeed, is the lynch-pin of our particular version of democracy – that each individual, within the limits of the law, has a right to do his own thing. Thus for society to say to a scientist, or a food processor, or a farmer, 'you do this and this, but not that' seems a betrayal of the democracy for which our society stands.

There is no easy way through the dilemma. Hold a gun to a scientist's or farmer's head, and tell him what to do, and you are not only asking a human being to behave as an ant, but you also kill the originality on which, in the end, you depend. Indeed, since the expert by definition knows more than the layman, it would be absurd for the layman to give the expert precise instruction.

The only way through the dilemma – and it is part of Mao Tse Tung's genius that he recognized this in the 1920s, 20 years before western physicists began to wonder whether they should or should not develop the atom bomb – is for the intellectuals, the experts, to identify totally with the society of which they are part; never to lose sight of the fact that they are part of their own society, and that society does not exist simply to provide a platform from which the intellectual can get a better view.

The Chinese, despite Mao, have not solved the dilemma. Their habit of sending intellectuals to work in the fields each year, to learn the problems of the masses, does seem a little crude. Not everyone wants to go anyway, and the peasants protest that the wheezy city workers get in the way. But at least the Chinese have recognized the magnitude of the dilemma. At least they recognize that by giving bright individuals their head – in accord with one principle of democracy – society tends to create an elite that has absolute power, because only it has the knowledge to do what is required; and that rule by elite is the complete antithesis of democracy.

The west has not recognized the magnitude of the dilemma, nor – despite recent requests from government that scientific research should be more 'relevant' to society's needs – has it taken effective steps to resolve it. This, I suggest, is a fundamental reason why the west has an agriculture, and a food-processing industry, that is a model of scientific purity but which does not serve the real needs of our society, nor respond to those of the world as a whole. And why we find men

E*

of outstanding intellect, trained at public expense, spending their time producing more luminous peas, or more heat-resistant packaging, when so many more useful things cry out to be done. We have fathered a race of Neros, fiddling sweetly while Rome burns.

And this leads us into the second major objection to rational agriculture – that it depends on central organization; that it requires people to work within prescribed constraints; that it turns creative humans into mere operatives; that it is, therefore, antithetical to democracy.

But democracy, like every other high-sounding political abstract, is a heterogeneous concept. It embraces the idea of individual freedom. It also embraces the idea of rule by popular consent – of policies that grow out of the wishes and aspirations and needs of the majority of people. These ideas are often in conflict.

I suggest that our western democracy has tended to put greater emphasis on the first – the individual freedom – than on the second. Rational agriculture requires a shift of emphasis. But it does not kill the concept of democracy. It merely requires that individual excellence and aspiration should not flourish at the expense of the aspirations of the majority: that, ideally, the individual's brilliance should find fulfilment by serving the needs of the majority.

The hybrid nature of 'democracy' gives rise to many paradoxes. Thus the self-sufficiency movement, eschewing control by faceless technocrats and demanding that each individual or family or commune should find salvation by hoeing its own patch, seems eminently democratic. Nobody tells anybody else what to do; everyone is free, except insofar as constrained by nature.

And since rational agriculture is rooted in a fair measure of individual self-reliance it finds valuable raw material in the techniques and philosophies developed and expounded by the self-sufficers. But John Seymour, author of the excellent *Fat of the Land*, and *Self Sufficiency*, argues in the first edition of the British magazine *Practical Self-Sufficiency* (there are several such publications in the US), that each family might reasonably acquire its own patch, dividing the country into self-supporting units. The splitting and re-splitting of land implied by this – ever more frenetic re-splitting, since such an arrangement is liable to produce an enormous population explosion – did not provide an adequate substitute for rational land reform in nineteenth-century Ireland; is proving disastrous in large areas of the Third World now; and was quickly abandoned by the Chinese, following a burst of over-enthusiasm, in the early years after their revolution.

Indeed, what appears to be the ultimate democratic gesture, the ultimate in individual expression, turns out merely to be anarchy. It has two possible consequences; either the system simply runs down, as it did in Ireland until the potato blight finally exposed the fundamental weakness, and caused mass famine and emigration; or a few energetic individuals, beginning innocently enough by forming co-operatives to counter the obvious shortcomings of the 'self-sufficient' units that cannot truly be self-sufficient, grow in power and wealth and begin the cycle of technology and capital all over again.

After all, at the turn of the eighteenth century Thomas Jefferson dreamed of a land of small farmers; and out of that pioneering spirit grew the juggernauting absurdity of modern US agriculture. His dream failed precisely because the mere aspiration of personal fulfilment was not enough; it needs a subtle and sophisticated political infrastructure if it is to flourish, and not allow a few to begin to dominate the many. It also lacked, partly because incompletely conceived, the industrial counterpoise that productive agriculture needs.

We saw in Chapter I how inadequate were eighteenth-century politics and biology in understanding the world's population problems. The eighteenth-century romantic concept of democracy is just as inappropriate here, primarily because the problems we now face are not those of the eighteenth century. But now, after 200 years of industrialization and Empire, we have the benefit of hindsight, if we care to learn from it.

Our defence of big business is also considered 'democratic', since the 'free' in 'free enterprise', is considered an essential aspect of more general individual freedom. But we have also come to believe – and the businessmen themselves half believe it – that big business is democratic also in the other sense – that it reflects the aspirations of the whole society. We saw, in the previous three chapters, how far that is from the truth. The food industry meets people's aspirations only insofar as it is profitable to do so; inconvenient aspirations it ignores, attempts to obliterate, or converts. It has enough power, through its control of production, sale, and advocacy, to bend public aspiration to its own ends.

Yet free enterprise has become the symbol of western democracy. We have come to believe that we are free, because we condone free enterprise. And when evil things are done in the cause of free enterprise – infant mortality increased in the Third World as a direct result of babymilk sales; fertilizer directed from India where it is needed to US golf courses where its use brings greater monetary return – we excuse them as inevitable side-effects of the democratic process. We have come to believe that if we demand our governments, or the United Nations, to curb these practices, that we are indirectly imperilling our own right to be free. We have not only delegated power to expert elites; we have made the elite of big business guardian of our concept of democracy.

But the alternative to the right-wing 'democratic' emphasis on individual freedom, seems, to westerners, to spell 'communism'. And, we are sometimes told, it is better to be dead than red.

But 'communism', like 'democracy', is also in practice a highly heterogenous concept. What strikes me about existing 'communist' states – even those under the imperial yoke of mother Russia – is how different they are one from another, and how much they have retained their 'national character'. China does not consider itself 'communist'; communism remains an ideal, that it does not claim yet to have achieved. It calls itself 'socialist'. But westerners consider it communist. Yet one of the deepest idealogical and methodological rifts in the world today is that between China and Russia. And modern Russia has not shuffled off the aspirations and traditions that caused the west to fear the Russian bear in the nineteenth century.

In short, I suggest that a Marxist economy would suit the needs of a rational agriculture, but not because I believe in the absolute rectitude of Marxist 'dogma', but because the kinds of constraints it imposes, and the kind of ideals it aspires to, seem to me to provide the most viable – to be the most likely to work – of all the possible alternatives. But the idea that to adopt such an economic base necessarily would turn Britain or the US into a carbon copy of Russia or China is absurd. It certainly has not turned either of those into a carbon copy of the other; it has simply allowed each to advance, but essentially they remain within the guidelines of their own tradition and history. There is far more to the west than capitalism; and what there is besides need not suffer from its demise.

It seems to me, therefore, that to attempt to adopt a communist ideal lock, stock and barrel would be absurd, primarily because there is no ideal to adopt. On the other hand, to deafen ourselves to the obvious arguments against capitalism, on the grounds that we must at all costs defend our own ill defined concept of democracy, and to fail to learn either from Marx, who first coherently expounded its theoretical shortcomings, or from the countries that have adopted a Marxist base – from their faults as well as their virtues – is to condemn us forever to a state in which the simple and rational things that need to be done cannot be done, because they do not fit in with the logic of our economy. We are on a Gadarene course, and we are taking much of the rest of the world with us; and no amount of technological genius, or opting out, can, in the end, compensate for that essential misdirection.

Let's end on a positive note. In a world where shortage of food is becoming the most conspicuous deficiency – as even Henry Kissinger acknowledged at the World Food Conference – we must take food seriously. In a society that values democracy, both in the sense of producing policies that reflect general aspiration, and in encouraging individual excellence, we need food policies, the crucial policies, in which everyone is involved. This does not mean everyone doing his own thing, for that would be disastrous. It does mean everyone having some intimation of why things are done. It does imply a society that does more than wait for the incumbent technocrats to dole out the next goodbie. It does mean education in the real sense – imparting knowledge of how food grows, and how people adapt what grows to their tastes – and not in the sense of indoctrination in the ways of industry.

It does imply more humility on the part of society's leaders, the politicians and scientists, and far more effort by people at large, because so long as people behave passively, they will be unable to resist the inexorable emergence of an energetic ruling elite. It does mean asking what our own idea of democracy really means: whether the businessman's distribution of ersatz meat, which affects people's lives more profoundly than the lifetime's work of the average elected politician, is truly characteristic of a democratic society. And it involves a more thoughtful appreciation of politics than is implied by the blanket dismissal of organization as 'communism'.

It implies a lot, then; quantum increase in knowledge, profound change of aspiration and mythology. But the prize, a well-fed people in a truly democratic world, is great; and the price of failure is total disaster from which our military and commercial strength cannot insulate us forever, and in the short term can save us only by delegating suffering elsewhere. No utopias. Nothing fancy. Just a political and economic framework in which it is 'realistic' to do simple things well.

References and Notes

CHAPTER I

1. United Nations, *Assessment of the World Food Situation*, 'Item 8 of the Provisional Agenda', World Food Conference, Rome, 1974. The figure of 460 million (para. 19) referred specifically to the Third World 'excluding the Asian centrally planned economies for which insufficient information is available.'

2. Gunnar Thorson, *Life in the Sea*, Weidenfeld and Nicolson, London, 1971, p. 206.

3. Gerald Leach, *Energy and Food Production*, IPC Science and Technology Press Ltd., Guildford, 1976.

4. John S. Steinhart and Carol E. Steinhart, 'Energy Use in the US Food System', *Science*, 1974, vol. 184, pp. 307–16.

5. Georg Borgstrom, *The Hungry Planet*, Collier Macmillan Ltd., London, 1967, p. xvi.

6. Frances Moore Lappé, *Diet for a Small Planet*, A Friends of the Earth/Ballantine Book, New York, 1971.

7. Don E. Dumond, *Science*, 1975, vol. 187, p. 713.

8. All the statistics in this list were freely bandied about at the World Food Conference (Rome, 1974). It would be tedious to trace all their origins. The Transnational Institute Report, *World Hunger: Causes and Remedies*, Amsterdam, October 1974, gives many similar examples, as does *The Party's Over*, Third World Publications, Birmingham, 1975.

9. C. R. Hensman, *Rich against Poor*, Penguin Books, Harmondsworth, 1971. President Johnson's speech, 9 October, 1968.

10. Reported by C. L. Sulsberger, *New York Times*, 11 January, 1967. (*Rich Against Poor*, p. 249).

11. References 11–15 quoted from R. Palme Dutt, *India Today*, Victor Gollancz Ltd., London, 1940.

12. Quoted by Sir William Willcocks, 'Lectures in the Ancient System of Irrigation in Bengal', University of Calcutta, 1930, pp. 18–19 (*India Today*, pp. 41–2).

13. Indian Industrial Commission Report, 1916–18, opening statement. (*India Today*, p. 42).

14. William Fullarton, M.P., 'A View of the English Interests in India', 1787. (*India Today*, p. 116).

15. H. H. Wilson, *History of British India*, vol. i, p. 385. (*India Today*, p. 125).

16. CIS Anti-Report No 11, *Unilever's World*, CIS, London, 1975. p. 9. Quoted from the *Evening Standard*, London, 8 May, 1972.

17. Georg Borgstrom, *World Food Resources*, International Textbook Co. Ltd., Aylesbury, Bucks, 1973.

18. World Development Movement, *End of an Illusion – Verdict on Unctad 3*, London, 1972.

CHAPTER II

19. This is illustrated in William Hinton's *Fan-shen*, a documentary of revolution in a Chinese village, Penguin Books, Harmondsworth, 1972.
20. For insight into the thinking behind national agricultural policies see Dr Gale Johnson's *World Agriculture in Disarray*, Macmillan Press Ltd., London, 1973.

CHAPTER III

21. Kenneth Blaxter, FRS, 'Can Britain Feed Itself?', *New Scientist*, 20 March, 1975, p. 697.
22. N. W. Pirie, *Food Resources: Conventional and Novel*, Penguin Books, Harmondsworth, 1969.
23. See N. W. Pirie 'Leaf Proteins: a beneficiary of tribulation', *Nature*, 1975, vol. 253, pp. 239–41.
24. See, for example, Philip Payne, 'Protein deficiency or starvation?', *New Scientist*, 7 November, 1974, p. 393.
25. Redcliffe Salaman, *The History and social influence of the Potato*, Cambridge University Press, Cambridge, 1949.
26. Ministry of Agriculture, Fisheries, and Food, *Manual of Nutrition*, HMSO, London, 1970.
27. I am particularly grateful to Dr Kenneth W. Giles and his colleague, Stuart M. Hobday, of Birkbeck College, University of London, for the insights contained in 'Improving the quality of plant proteins' – regrettably unpublished at the time of writing.
28. J. F. W. Von Bulow and Johanna Dobereiner, *Proceedings of the National Academy of Sciences of the USA*, 1975, vol. 72, p. 2389.
29. C. E. Fogg, Leeuwenhoek lecture, Royal Society, 1968. Reported in the *Proceedings of the Royal Society*, Series B, 1969, vol. 173, pp. 175–89.
30. I am grateful to Michael Allaby, of Friends of the Earth, for the statistics on protein yields per acre.
31. H. C. Pereira (Chief Scientist to the Ministry of Agriculture, Fisheries and Food), 'Research and Development for Britain's future food supplies', lecture given at the Twelfth British Weed Control Conference, Brighton, 19 November, 1974.
32. Russell Kyle, *Meat Production in Africa. The case for new domestic species*, University of Bristol, England, 1972.
33. K. L. Blaxter, 'Deer Farming', *Scottish Agriculture*, Winter 1971/72, pp. 225–30.
34. Dr Orskov is a scientist at the Rowett Research Institute, Aberdeen, Scotland. Information conveyed in personal communication.
35. R. T. Berg and R. M. Butterfield, 'Growth of Meat Animals' in *Meat*, ed. D. J. A. Cole and R. A. Laurie, Butterworths, London, 1975, p. 13.

36. Donald Naismith, 'Bottle feeding makes you fat . . . and the children too', *World Medicine*, 13 March, 1974, p. 26.
37. See Michael and Sheilagh Crawford, *What We Eat Today*, Neville Spearman Ltd., London, 1972.
38. See John Yudkin, *Pure, White and Deadly*, David-Poynter Ltd., London, 1972.

CHAPTER IV

39. Ernest Hollings comments in *The Case Against Hunger:* 'We no longer allow farmers to give their livestock and poultry anything but the best formulated feeds.' (Quoted from Frances Moore Lappé, *Diet for a Small Planet*, p. 9.)
40. See, for example, Margaret Capstick, *The Economies of Agriculture*, George Allen and Unwin Ltd., London, 1970.

CHAPTER V

41. Donald D. McLaren, 'The Great Protein Fiasco', *Lancet*, 1974, vol. 2, p. 93.
42. See, for example P. V. Sukhatme, *British Journal of Nutrition*, 1970, vol. 24, pp. 477–87; and J. C. Waterlow and P. R. Payne, 'The protein gap', *Nature*, 1975, vol. 258, pp. 113–17.
43. Bruce R. Stillings, 'World Supplies of Animal Protein', *Proteins in Human Nutrition*, ed. J. W. G. Porter and B. A. Rolls, Academic Press, London, 1973, p. 13.
44. See, in particular, T. L. Cleave, G. D. Campbell, and N. S. Painter, *Diabetes, Coronary Thrombosis and the Saccharine Disease*, 2nd ed., John Wright & Sons Ltd., Bristol, 1969; and *Refined Carbohydrates and Disease*, ed. D. P. Burkitt, and H. C. Trowell, Academic Press, London, 1975.
45. Hugh Trowell, 'Obesity in the Western World', *Plant Foods for Man*, 1974, vol. 1, pp. 157–68.
46. See papers by M. A. Eastwood, and K. W. Heaton, in *Fibre Deficiency and Colonic Disorders*, ed. R. W. Reilly and J. B. Kirsner, Plenum Press, New York, 1975. (Proceedings of a conference held in Chicago, May 1974.)
47. Denis Burkitt, et al., *Lancet*, 1972, vol. 2, p. 1408.
48. K. Heaton, *Lancet*, 1973, vol. 2, p. 1418.
49. Frank M. Sacks, et al., 'Plasma lipids and lipoproteins in vegetarians and controls', *The New England Journal of Medicine*, 1975, vol. 292, pp. 1148–51.
50. John Yudkin, *Pure, White and Deadly*, pp. 23–8. The author speaks of two 'food revolutions': the first, neolithic, including a switch to a high-carbohydrate diet; the second, the outcome of increased food refinement.
51. John Yudkin, *This Slimming Business*, Penguin Books, Harmondsworth, rev. ed., 1965.

CHAPTER VI
52. G. Teleki, *The Predatory Behaviour of Wild Chimpanzees*, Buknell University Press, Lewisburg, Pennsylvania, 1973.
53. S. C. Struen, *Science*, 1975, vol. 187, p. 755.
54. Hugo and Jane Goodall Van Lawick, *Innocent Killers*, Collins, London, 1970, p. 26 et seq.
55. *The Times*, 17 May, 1974.
56. Jean-Anthelme Brillat-Savarin, *The Philosopher in the Kitchen*, trans. Anne Drayton, Penguin Books, Harmondsworth, 1970 (original: *La Physiologie du gout*, published 1825).

CHAPTER VII
57. Jane Grigson, *Good Things*, Penguin Books, Harmondsworth, 1973.
58. Robert Carrier, *The Robert Carrier Cook Book*, Sphere Books Ltd., London, 1967, p. 466.
59. For comparable approaches see Dorothy Hartley, *Food in England*, Macdonald, London, 1954.
60. See, for example, Nika Standen Hazelton, *The Swiss Cookbook*, Atheneum, New York, 1967.

CHAPTER VIII
61. James Thomson, 'Should modern food carry a government health warning?', *World Medicine*, 24 September, 1975, pp. 74–81.

CHAPTER IX
62. Royal Society Discussion Meeting, 'Food Technology in the 1980s'. 23 and 24 May, 1974.
63. Meg Dods, quoted in F. Marian McNeill, *The Scots Kitchen*, Blackie & Son Ltd., London, 2nd ed., 1963, p. 17.
64. *Birds Eye Annual Review*, 1974, p. 4.
65. Quoted in publicity material distributed by Barrett Card Associates Limited, London, on behalf of Ranks Hovis McDougall.
66. Fay Maschler, 'Hard to swallow, my mouthful of make-believe', *Evening Standard*, 5 March, 1975.
67. *Can Britain Feed Itself*, p. 34, Kenneth Melanby, Merlin Press, London, 1975.
68. Michael Allaby, Colin Blythe and Colin Hines, *Losing Ground*, Earth Resources Research Ltd., London, 1974, pp. 28–9.
69. *Meat* (see reference 35) p. 15.
70. Frazer Imrie, 'Single-cell protein from agricultural wastes', *New Scientist*, 22 May, 1975, pp. 458–60.

CHAPTER X
71. 'I don't associate the word "unnecessary" with "advertising expenditure" because advertising is almost the most essential expendi-

ture" for a company like ours.' Kenneth Webb, chairman of Birds Eye Foods Ltd., reported in *Birds Eye Annual Review*, 1974, p. 17.
72. For example, Andrew Hutton, 'No Grain of Comfort from US', *Pan* (newspaper of the World Food Conference in Rome, 1974) 16 November, 1974.

CHAPTER XI
73. 'Recent research has shown that frozen foods are among the most consistently profitable items for retailers.' *Birds Eye Annual Review*, 1971, p. 28.
74. Arnold Spicer, 'Synthetic Proteins for Human and Animal Consumption', *The Veterinary Record*, 30 October, 1971, pp. 482–7.
75. Hugh Geach, *New Internationalist*, August, 1973.
76. Mike Muller, *The Baby Killer*, War on Want, London, March 1974.
77. Editorial, 'Synthetic Foods', *The Lancet*, 1972, vol. 2, p. 1012.
78. Dorothy Hollingsworth, *New Scientist*, 23 May, 1974, p. 499.
79. *Bread: An assessment of the British food industry*, Technology Assessment Consumerism Centre, Intermediate Publishing, 1974.
80. *World Medicine*, 5 June, 1974, p. 27.

CHAPTER XII
81. According to C. R. Hensman 700,000 of the four million who founded the independent USA were black slaves: and the total removed over four centuries may be as high as 50 million.
82. 'Doctors join vets in drive to combat rural ills', *Farmers Weekly*, 26 December, 1969.
83. Dr Bernard Dixon, editor *New Scientist*, personal communication.
84. Ivan D. Illich, *Tools for Conviviality*, Harper and Row Publishers, Inc., New York, 1973.
85. Ross Hume Hall, in *Food for Nought*, Harper and Row, New York, 1974, admirably reviews the process whereby technique has taken over from common sense.
86. Thomas Szasz expanded this theme in a symposium on genetic engineering, at Davos, Switzerland, October 1974. Reported in *World Medicine*, 4 December, 1974, pp. 17–29.

Index